Praise for *States of Being*

Everyone needs a coach, but very few people get a coach who listens, pushes, and empowers you to solve your own problems. In *States of Being*, Belans mixes cutting-edge neuroscience with timeless philosophical thought, all while stimulating your mind, guiding your heart, and magnifying your soul. She has beautifully captured her methods in a powerful, practical, and inspiring book. *States of Being* might be viewed as a book for education leaders in US schools, but it is actually relevant to anyone who wants to support another human being to improve, believe, shine, and give.

—GAURAV SINGH, Founder and CEO,
321 Education Foundation (Mumbai, India)

States of Being empowers us to coach others from a place of love, compassion, and empathy. Linda's thoughtful approach to coaching spans far beyond this practice. She teaches us to honor and recognize the humanity in others, the adults we lead and the students we have the privilege of serving. I am a better human being in the world as a result.

—CONSTANCE RANAE JONES, CEO, Noble Schools

When I think of someone who demonstrates unwavering love, leadership, and commitment to students on the margins, I think of Dr. B. Her *States of Being* is an extraordinary work that helps make it possible for hardworking students of all backgrounds to succeed.

—CALVON JONES, M.Div. (Yale University), Associate Pastor to Children and
Youth, Trinity United Church of Christ (Chicago)

Every student in every classroom deserves to be taught by teachers and leaders who model the work presented in *States of Being*. As I work with leaders across the country to practice the transformational work of Dr. Belans, I see a new light in people's eyes when they realize that urgency, rigor, and humanity can—and must—coexist so that *all* who enter the building can thrive.

—JEANA MARINELLI, Leadership Coach

States of Being is an indispensable guide for teachers at all levels and in all environments. Its powerful coaching model speaks to contemporary challenges in the classroom, particularly racism and sexism. It has been of particular value to me in my work with university graduate students.

—GERALD STEINACHER, Ph.D., Professor of History, Holocaust educator, and author of *Nazis on the Run: How Hitler's Henchmen Fled Justice*

STATES OF BEING

LEADERSHIP COACHING FOR EQUITABLE SCHOOLS

Linda Belans, Ed.D.

Circle the Moon Press
Durham, NC

First edition, 2020

Reproduction of this book or these materials for an entire school system is strictly forbidden. Individual coaches, school leaders, and classroom teachers can find one-page coaching models and additional resources at www.statesofbeing.net

Requests for permission to reproduce material should be sent to linda@lindabelans.com

"Come to the Edge" from *New Numbers*, Cape, 1969, copyright © Christopher Logue, 1969. Reprinted by permission of David Godwin Associates, Ltd.

Cover photo: *Street Fossil*, by Jim Lee, www.bambooturtle.com
The Ginkgo biloba is the oldest living tree in the world. Commonly found on city streets, it is a symbol of resilience.
Cover design by BuzBooks
Interior book design by Van-Garde Imagery, Inc

Library of Congress Cataloging-in-Publication Data
Names: Belans, Linda, author
Title: States of Being: Leadership Coaching for Equitable Schools / Linda Belans
Description: Durham, North Carolina : Circle the Moon Press, [2020] | Includes bibliographical references.
Identifiers: Library of Congress Control Number: 2020905207 | ISBN 9781734559200 (paperback) | ISBN 9781734559217 (e-book)
Subjects: LCSH: Leadership coaching--Education. | Equitable Schools. | Educators. | Educational Coaching--Equity. | Teacher Development. | Assets-based Coaching. | Self-help.

For Keith Burnam
April 15, 1980 – November 17, 2016

Seeker of truth. Rule breaker. One who
asked the hard question, because it was the
question that needed to be asked.
One who challenged authority for the
sake of his students. The man whose mere
presence created a sense of belonging for them.
His spirit continues to infuse me.

And
for my grandchildren

TABLE OF CONTENTS

Foreword by Donnell K. Bailey iii

Prelude xi

Chapter 1:   The Why: Discovering, Developing, and Teaching
              the States of Being 1

Chapter 2:   See the Higher Self (Coach to Assets) 17

Chapter 3:   Honor Story (Listen) 37

Chapter 4:   Be Curious (Ask Nonjudgmental Questions) 43

Chapter 5:   Be Bold (Hold Their Hand While You Hold
              Their Feet to the Fire). 51

Chapter 6:   Be Present (Remain Unattached to Outcome) 67

Chapter 7:   Be Compassionate (Walk in Their Shoes) 81

Chapter 8:   Interrupt Patterns (Notice Repetition) 89

Chapter 9:   Acknowledge Mystery (Trust Intuition). 99

Chapter 10:   Quiet the Ego (Check In before Checking Out) . . . 109

Chapter 11:   Appreciate That Everyone Has a Piece of the
              Truth (Gather Perspectives). 119

Chapter 12:   Imbue Others with Their Own Intelligence
               (Help Them Connect the Dots). 131

               Coda 141

               Last Look 149

               Acknowledgments 151

               Bibliography 155

Foreword

"DONNELL, MAN, YOU'RE NOT THE same Donnell anymore, what happened?" A former teacher said these words to me in eighth grade when we ran into each other at the second-floor printer. He said it casually, kindly, but with slight amazement. He certainly meant it as a compliment, and at the time I probably took it as one.

Looking back at this moment now, however, I see a more fraught reality. There is an expectation of failure that surrounds young men of color in education, especially in high-poverty schools. We enter a system where being disciplined is the norm, a system that lays the groundwork for either future incarceration or a future life of oppression and low expectations. Success is the aberration. The assumption is that in order to succeed, or even to avoid punishment, we have to change who we fundamentally are: "You're not the same Donnell." My teacher's offhand comment inadvertently affirms this dangerous way of thinking and demonstrates why Dr. Linda Belans's States of Being work is, in the words of Stephen Covey, not just *merely important* but *wildly important*.

In one sense, the teacher was right; I wasn't the same Donnell.

When I had been in his class just a year earlier, I had spent most of my time in suspension or "on the bench" (as one form of discipline was called). When we met at the printer, I had begun winning leadership awards, and the suspensions were almost entirely behind me. In reality, however, I was the same Donnell I had always been. Only now, there had been a crucial shift in my circumstances that changed both how others saw me and how I saw my own potential. That shift came in the form of a mentor who began coaching to my assets. He saw my higher self and asked me to do the same. Jared Lamb was my math teacher, my track coach, and the school leader, and unbeknownst to me, he was being coached by Dr. B in the States of Being.

Addressing behavior with constant discipline and punishments is deficits-based training. It's probably the most pervasive and least effective style of education and training many students encounter. I was stuck in this rut of deficits and discipline until I met Jared. However, had Jared focused solely on helping me change my behavior in order to avoid suspension, that might have been effective in the short term, but such a narrow, results-oriented focus could never have been transformational in the way that Dr. B's assets-based coaching is.

One incident, in particular, stands out when I consider how Jared helped me see my higher self. My behavior had landed me in Saturday school detention. As I was sitting in the classroom I began to internalize the environment and what it meant to be there. I felt horrible because I had to wear an embarrassing t-shirt that publicly shamed me for the, in my opinion, small talking disruption I made in class. After sitting in detention for a few hours I wrote the words "I hate myself" on my t-shirt. When Jared, who was on Saturday detention duty, came by and noticed the words on my shirt, he was shocked and I think, to a degree, hurt, because it was not the way he saw me.

He motioned for me to follow him into a nearby classroom and asked why I had written those words. After I replied, we just sat there for a moment, then he asked me to go to the whiteboard and pick up a marker. He told me to list all the positive and good character traits I saw in myself. At first, I thought this was a pointless exercise, but with Jared's encouragement, I began to write things like "integrity," "leader," "optimistic." He had me write my strengths from left to right until the entire whiteboard was filled. It was exhausting. Afterwards we both sat back and began to read them aloud, reinforcing the activity and laughing at some. I didn't know it at the time but this was an activity that pulled out my higher self. I could see a lot of these things in myself. I just had to name them. I had to learn to recognize them and nurture them.

Was this the defining *big* moment that changed the path of my school career? I'm not sure. But I know it was part of the process, and I know it was my last time in Saturday detention. I had a new perception of myself, because I knew I had to live by the character traits I wrote on the board. I trusted and knew that Jared Lamb would hold me accountable to them, and that there would now be no excuses not to live up to them, not to honor them.

About the same time, another crucial mentor came into my life. Linda Belans, then Director of the KIPP Leadership Coaching Program, came to my social studies class as part of a site visit. I was the classroom ambassador, which meant I was the student who greeted her and explained what we were studying. During this brief exchange, she asked me what I wanted to be when I grew up. I was 14, and it was the first time anyone in a school had ever seriously asked me this question. Imagine going from kindergarten through eighth grade without being asked this fundamental question, without being asked to consider a future. I remember this because it was the first time I had ever given an answer.

I said, "President of the United States." In my mind this was the vision that I had back then; I was taking the long view. Plus, it was

2008, and Barack Obama had shown that a Black man could run for president. The idea of the long view is a crucial part of Dr. B's work, and that question by definition takes a long view—it's an assets-based question—*what do you want to be when you grow up?* It sounds like such a simple, ordinary question, and for many children in this country it is. Indeed, it's such a common question for these children that after a few years of eliciting dreams, the query becomes boring and even eye-roll inducing for young students. "What do you want to be when you grow up?" implies a world of possibilities, an access to privileges, networks, and opportunities that is casual and simply taken for granted by many young students in this country. But there are too many other children who rarely hear this question, children who stand, virtually unseen, outside that "normal" world of access. They are trapped in a corrupt educational system defined by racial segregation, wealth inequality, and poverty-structured neighborhoods. They are not asked to consider a future of accomplishment and privilege.

Dr. B understood the empowering nature of her question even before I did. She was inviting me to imagine a world where I had access. I realized I wanted those possibilities. A chance meeting with her in the streets of New Orleans later that evening solidified the invitation. She gave me her card and told me to follow up. I believed her invitation was genuine, so I did follow up, and she has been a coach, mentor, and dear friend ever since.

The assets-based States of Being mentoring that I received from Jared and Dr. B changed the trajectory of my life. I went on to become middle-school council president and won the class's leadership award. I earned admission to an elite private high school, where I was suddenly thrust into a world of privilege and entitlement for the first time in my life, but I held fast to my coaching and became class president my first year there. After high school, I became the first member of my family to attend college and was the first Black student elected president of the student body at Franklin & Marshall College. I interned for U.S. Representative Joseph Cao, U.S. Senator Mary Landrieu, and in the Obama White House. I was also asked to join the KIPP New Orleans Board of Directors and am the youngest board member and first alumnus ever to serve. Now, I am Executive Assistant to the Vice President of Enrollment Management and Dean of Admissions at Tulane University, a Tier 1 research university in my hometown, and where I have just been accepted into the inaugural class of the Master of Public Administration program.

Having gone from school suspension to school board, I know first hand why we must bring assets- and equity-based coaching to *every* student in *every* school. The work of equity requires us to take the long view. It's shortsighted to focus only on immediate results, such as fewer disciplinary problems or higher test scores. We need transformational change—institutionally and individually. We need teachers who can connect students to their higher selves, and we need school leaders who can do the same for the teachers. We need an educational system that fosters a sense of belonging in our students so that, no matter what their background, they can envision themselves in positions of privilege, leadership, and power.

For students stuck in systems that reinforce racial segregation and poverty, the lack of access and belonging cannot be overstated. With hindsight, I can see that many of the qualities and impulses that landed me in suspension are the same traits I call on now as a leader. When I felt insecure or out of place as a young student, I'd try to create camaraderie by making jokes or talking (in the halls, in class, in places where my contributions were deemed "disruptive"). I know now I was trying to find commonalities so I could belong. By seeing my higher self, Jared helped me understand that my desire to create a sense of belonging extended beyond myself and that I could channel my "disruptions" into leadership. Dr. B's coaching helped me identify my values. What's clearer to me now (one of her favorite wrap-up questions) is that I want to create an inclusive, educational, and safe environment conducive for young people to develop into their full selves and thrive.

Recently, I had the opportunity to mentor a group of young students in much the same way that Dr. B has always done for me. It was Campus Preview Day at Tulane, and I noticed a Black mother and three of her children who looked like they needed some direction. I asked if I could help, and serendipitously they were looking for the chemistry lab, which was where I was headed for the "open house" portion of the day. We walked into the huge classroom together, and I told them to feel free to look around as long as they liked. I had learned on the walk over that two of the woman's three children were high school seniors and excellent students, and the third was not yet in high school.

Almost as soon as we walked into the classroom, I could sense a major disconnect. They were in a classroom with no explanation of why, and what they were seeing was just what was in front of them: lab stations, glass bottles, funky chemistry equations written on the boards, but nothing to help personalize this sterile environment. I could see they were becoming disengaged. I could see the wheels spinning in their heads that this all seemed kind of pointless. It was at that moment that I spotted a couple of white lab coats, and the light bulb went off in my head. "Hey," I called out, "want to try on some lab coats?!" One by one I got them fitted. In the coats, their energy changed. They were excited. When the young Black man tried his coat on, it fit him like it was *his* coat. He nodded his head and said, "Yeah, this does look good on me." When we went back into the lab section of the classroom, there was a difference, a huge difference. Their eyes lit up; they were engaging with the classroom: They put on pairs of orange gloves, picked up and examined the beakers, and posed for pictures. Now, they could envision themselves being in a chemistry class at a prestigious and highly selective university.

In many ways the writing of the traits on the board and the putting on of lab coats isn't so different. Both seek to open a world of possibilities that a deficits-based framework had made seem impossible. When we operate from an assets-based framework, we are able to see the talents and gifts our students have to offer. And to be clear, this spark exists in each of our students. We have to be part of creating a place of belonging that will allow them to be fearless and vulnerable in order to become their best selves. Whether a student is at an elite private school or a low-income public school, what makes the difference is whether a student is consistently viewed through a lens of deficits or whether the student is given a chance each day to get it right. That is why it's so critical to see the States of Being as a model that can be applied across systems, not just in individual schools or by certain school leaders. The focus should be on ensuring that our whole K–12 educational system—charter, public, or private—is providing an equitable education to all children and delivering on best outcomes for their lives.

I often feel that Dr. B has genuinely been in my life for no other reason than to see me become my best self. I say this first because as I continue to grow into adulthood and leadership, I'm learning just how very rare this is—when someone is invested in you for you, not for her own return on investment. I had absolutely no idea who I was meeting when I met Dr. B, nor did I know we would keep in touch for so long. I've learned so much from her in big moments and in small lessons around leadership, guiding principles, research and data, and voice. At every turn she has helped me to become a better version of myself by teaching me the power of story, narrative, and identity. When we first met she used to call me her "youngest coachee," and I wear that label like a badge of honor. Here she was coaching school leaders from around the country, and she made time to have calls with me. When I have needed her, especially in some very critical moments in my life, she has always been there. Dr. B has been a joy to learn from and get to know as a student, as her youngest coachee, and now as the writer of this foreword to her life's work. I'm thankful to experience a full-circle moment with such an incredible mentor and dear friend.

So I will conclude this foreword the way Dr. B and I have ended every coaching call over the past 12 years, by answering the question: What is clearer to you now?

We need bold, assets-based leadership in order to leverage the power of our schools and institutions to bring people together and to create a path forward for a more just and equitable society. The States of Being model is urgent because we need urgent school leaders to meet the daily challenges students face around systems that have failed them and their families for too long. This framework is critically important, because so many students who live their lives at the intersection of race, class, and power have experienced how structural barriers systematically shape outcomes for underrepresented people in very predictable ways. And while these structural challenges exist, the States of Being can help to unstructure them by investing in our leaders so we may improve the futures of the students we serve.

—Donnell K. Bailey

Prelude

What's Clearer to Me

We ask so much of teachers and leaders who begin their careers with a fierce urgency to "straighten the crooked room" of education, to borrow Melissa Harris-Perry's apt phrasing. But many burn out and leave under the weight of their heavy, unsupported dream. There is little to nothing that is equitable about the resources afforded to most schools located in high-poverty communities—from classroom size, to money for social workers, facilities, professional development, health care, and nutritious meals. There aren't enough textbooks or desks. As a result, student outcomes in these schools are historically at the bottom of the test and learning scale. To put it in stark terms, predominantly white school districts receive $23 billion more in funding than districts that serve mostly students of color, according to a recent report by the educational think tank EdBuild. These are communities where privilege never sees the light of day, where poverty dampens hope and diminishes opportunity. And, paradoxically, where complex issues of race and equity are rarely wrestled with.

To be clear, even if schools in poverty-burdened communities were given that same $23 billion, it might be an equal allocation, but it would not be equitable because these students start out behind and need more resources just to catch up. *Equity* means giving everyone what they need in order to be successful. This definition has implications beyond the financial. It speaks to a panoply of interwoven issues that include how beliefs translate into action—an entire approach to how we view and treat students and each other. It begins with leadership, which will be explored and addressed throughout the book.

When I first began researching this material for my doctorate about nine years ago, the dissertation title was "States of Being: The What, Why, and How of Coaching Urgent School Leaders." I used the word *urgent* rather than the common term *urban* because the work of educating children living in structured poverty—whether in decidedly urban centers like New York City and Mumbai or in more rural areas like the Mississippi Delta—is critical and demanding, sometimes a matter of life or death.

Urgency has taken on new meaning for me since the 2016 elections. We are experiencing a sanctioned vilification of the Other, and attendant policies or threats of policies to codify it. Although many perceive that these policies and practices signify a recent or sudden culture shift, the reality is that the election simply exposed the racism, sexism, genderism, inequities, and poverty that have long been festering beneath the surface.

And, yet, I am cautiously optimistic. First, because as a woman in the eighth decade of life, I have been witness to dark political and societal times that we, as a nation, have emerged from—often for the better. We do this when we collectively understand the What, our vision and values; when we vividly communicate the Why, to influence others; and when we implement the How through a strong and clear strategy. As I write this, teachers—entire school districts across the nation—are taking to the streets demanding change. School lead-

ers—seasoned and emerging—are beginning to ask the most necessary questions: What are schools for, and how do we create them?

What's clearer to me is that we are called on to create schools
where kindness and academic rigor can and must coexist. Where we
have to care as much, if not more, about our students' and teachers' aspirations as we do about test scores and data. There must be a
deliberate, clear-eyed practice of infusing equity into every decision
and move that leaders make. We need to actively teach these skills,
and the language of these skills, to all who have a stake in educating
our students as we imagine them into their futures. If we are going to
deliver on our promises to all of our children, we have to discipline
ourselves to see the higher self in the struggling first-year teacher as
well as in the emerging leader, bus drivers, custodians, board members—anyone who has contact with our students. If we are going
to save democracy, we have to collectively imagine and plan for the
kind of world we want our children to inherit and inhabit. And we
have to create schools that address this vision. There is too much at
stake. This is why I created the States of Being—to offer a coaching
response to these pressing questions: What are schools for? How do
we manifest them?

How to Use This Book

This book uses actual coaching sessions to describe and model coaching techniques or intentions that can be integrated into the work of
people in leadership positions who manage others in schools, districts, or regions.[1] States of Being can be employed whether coaches
are hired externally or work internally. The practice is adaptable for
public schools, charter schools, private schools, independent schools,

---

1. The coaching sessions documented here are all derived from actual sessions, with permission of the leaders whose names were changed. Occasionally, small details were altered to
protect the leader's identity and honor confidentiality.

and anywhere leadership coaching is used, including arenas outside the educational world, such as nonprofits or the corporate world. The States of Being described in this book are tools derived from (1) deconstructing the coaching sessions I have been engaged in for more than 25 years; and (2) listening closely to the coaches I have hired, developed, worked with, and learned with (and from). I also conducted surveys of about one thousand school leaders who have worked with these coaches.

The book offers two dialogues: external and internal. I deconstruct the external dialogues I have had with leaders that I coach, and then I share and analyze the internal dialogue I have with myself during the sessions. The use of my internal dialogue is one of the ways in which this book is different from other books on leadership coaching, and its inclusion was essential to me from the beginning. It is critical to notice what's happening to us as we coach. We must be aware of our triggers, fears, anxieties, biases, and so on.

I use the term *leader*, but the process can and should be used with teachers, staff, and students as well so that a culture of coaching is established throughout the school or district.

Pronouns toggle among *she*, *he*, and *they* to be inclusive.

There are 11 States of Being. Each State of Being has its own chapter in a What (vision), Why (influence), and How (strategy) format. The What is the particular State of Being. The Why is the case for it. The How is a brief description, followed by an illustrative meditation or story on the practice. There is a coaching model at the end of each State's chapter. Additional resources, including an abbreviated, one-page version of these coaching models, can be found at www.statesofbeing.net. You can print these models as needed and keep them on hand as a quick reference tool.

Each State of Being has a long form—"What" ("How")—and a short form, usually just the "What" or just the "How." So, for example, See the Higher Self (Coach to Assets) tells you both what you're trying to accomplish and how you're going to do it. As familiarity and comfort with the States increases, it may only be necessary to refer to the What (i.e., See the Higher Self, Be Curious, Honor Story) or the How (Coach to Assets, Ask Nonjudgmental Questions, Listen). In order to draw your attention to the way the States of Being permeate the work and also to demonstrate how they often work together, the States and the language that refers to using the States will often be italicized throughout the book (i.e., "When I started *coaching to the teacher's assets*, it was easier for me to see how to *imbue her with her own intelligence*").

States of Being are designed to liberate you as a coach, to bring your full, authentic self to the process, just as we want leaders to do. They are a set of intentions that enable you to be nimble and adaptive, rather than a prescription of what coaching should be or look like. The States invite you to begin with self by being aware of what's happening to you internally as you are engaging with the leader. This assures that we are coaching to the leader's needs, rather than letting our own issues, attitudes, biases, and the way *we* would do things, infect the process. We achieve this by practicing the States of Being that will best serve not only the leader's individual circumstance but also our own internal responses to it. By the end of this book it will be clear that like tools in a toolbox, the States have specific and overlapping uses. As you become more familiar with the What, the How, and the Why of each State, you will develop an intuitive sense of which States to call on at any given moment in a coaching session.

There are three constant States of Being that are the hallmark of every coaching session: (1) See the Higher Self; (2) Honor Story; and (3) Be Curious. These three States make use of fundamental practices that build the necessary trust for developing and sustaining successful coaching relationships. This trilogy sets the tone and landscape for self-discovery through identifying and leveraging strengths that the leader brings to leadership. It helps the coach mine data through the way we engage with their stories.

Be Bold sits right under the trilogy. Sometimes, we have to interrupt patterns that interfere with a leader's work, or hold a mirror up so he can see himself as others might see him. This is a State of Being that coaches have to work with compassionately without dismantling trust. We weave and glide among the States of Being, depending on what the leader presents.

The 11 States of Being → What (How)

1. See the Higher Self (Coach to Assets)

2. Honor Story (Listen)

3. Be Curious (Ask Nonjudgmental Questions)

4. Be Bold (Hold Their Hand While You Hold Their Feet to the Fire)

5. Be Present (Remain Unattached to Outcome)

6. Be Compassionate (Walk in Their Shoes)

7. Interrupt Patterns (Notice Repetition)

8. Acknowledge Mystery (Trust Intuition)

9. Quiet the Ego (Check In before Checking Out)

10. Appreciate That Everyone Has a Piece of the Truth (Gather Perspectives)

11. Imbue Others with Their Own Intelligence (Help Them Connect the Dots)

On their own, however, States of Being are not enough. It is also essential that we boldly delve into our own cultural, racial, gender biases, and identities. (We can do this through organizations or programs whose work is dedicated to dismantling racism and LGBTQ oppression.) We must commit to regularly interrogating our interactions through these lenses throughout our coaching lives. Otherwise, we run the risk of denying the humanity of the people we coach. Without continuous self-examination, we will be unable to coach leaders to examine their own biases and beliefs, and those that exist within their schools and communities. To help infuse this work into coaching and leading, here are Seven Essential Equity Questions (7EQs) developed through research, and in collaboration with trusted colleagues who are on the national forefront of anti-racist work. The 7EQs are designed to create a sense of belonging, a fundamental human need that fuels our aspirations, reduces stress, increases a sense of well-being, and impacts intellectual achievement. I include "creating a sense of belonging" as one of the 7EQs so that we are actively and intentionally coaching and leading with this end in mind. The 7EQs, intertwined throughout the book, help us stay focused on creating compassionate and equitable schools.

The 7EQs

1. How are we beginning with self to examine our implicit and explicit biases?

2. What does an equitable school look, feel, and sound like for students, staff, and families?

3. How are we creating a sense of belonging?

4. How are we noticing and acting on opportunities to interrupt systemic and structured racism?

5. What are we doing to create conditions for students, staff, and families to feel free to be authentic?

6. What are we doing to inhibit conditions for students, staff, and families to feel free to be authentic?

7.   How are we actively creating equitable schools, organizations, and communities?

When leaders and their staff don't actively wrestle with the 7EQs, or other similar investigations, schools can become institutions anchored in control and oppression rather than structure and love. School policies run the risk of being created and implemented through unexamined lenses with unintended outcomes. Teachers can confuse consequences with punishment, and normal child developmental behavior with cultural biases. Without continuous examination of biases and beliefs, we risk imposing cultural irrelevancy and reinforcing harmful, internalized inequality. It creates environments where a sense of belonging for girls of color can be undermined when their achievement is overlooked, and their rate of suspension can be 10 to 12 times higher than that of white girls, according to a study by Kimberlé Williams Crenshaw for the African American Policy Forum and the Center for Intersectionality and Social Policy Studies. It sets up situations where pushback to unfairness is viewed as rude by students of color, but as questioning by white students. Without engaging in the work of equity, school employees can view and treat students and their families as Other. They can create unnecessary tensions between parent/guardian and child by placing final-straw requests on families living in back-breaking poverty. For example, schools steeped in equity practices wouldn't dream of asking parents to take time from their hourly-wage work to sit with their child all day to make sure they behave. It's painful to imagine that there are schools that implement this policy. Coaching can help leaders find equitable practices by regularly working with the 7EQs.

It is essential that we seriously, intentionally, and continuously commit to the work of equity if we are going to help leaders create schools and support communities that lift up our students and their families.

What Coaches Do and Don't Do

Coaching intermingles science and art. The States of Being are the science; the art is the ability to move and dance with agility among them. In this complex, structured improvisational duet, the coach accesses intuition rooted in experience to maintain a steady beat when the leader struggles to find their rhythm. The coach holds the space when they spiral up or down and continuously notices and monitors herself so that she can be fully present, clear, and responsive to the leader's movement.

As a dancer, I experience coaching as a structured-contact improvisational duet that depends on interdependence. There is something mysterious about what happens between two people engaged in this dance, one that requires us to be responsive to stimuli. We have to be comfortable with and practiced at taking risks, concentrating and persisting, understanding how our partner's moves affect our own, able to sense what our partner is expressing and knowing how to respond. Effective coaches are comfortable in intellectual, spiritual, and emotional arenas.

This is why *coaching is not a profession for everyone.* The practice requires us to be keenly self-aware, to park our egos at the door, and to relinquish power. Coaches are compassionate, attentive, deliberate, ethical thought and heart partners. Coaches have to have disciplined fidelity to confidentiality, as agreed upon, and be more patient than we might have ever imagined we could be. We have to be satisfied with small and big insights, with major and minor transformation. We must be comfortable with stasis and sometimes regression.

Our job is to help leaders see, understand, engage with, and deconstruct what they do well and learn how to translate their strengths and talents to address the challenges that keep them up at night. Our work is to provide leaders with a safe, confidential place to lay down their worries and fears—to hold the space for them while they investigate the edges of safety and uncertainty. To help them see their impact on others and the impact of others on them. To help them problem-solve, articulate their vision and mission, and anchor their decisions in their Why. To help them learn how to create an end-in-mind, as well as delegate and see it through. To see themselves and their schools as part of the larger community they inhabit. To learn to live with ambiguity. To help assuage the loneliness that comes with leadership. To be their mirrors and their kind truth-tellers, to see them with clear eyes while being their advocates and part of their team. Our job is not to make them perfect; it is to build on what they bring.

When we're experienced, it can be so tempting to tell the leader what to do. That's closer to what consultants often do: they are invited to the workplace to assess it and make objective recommendations. A primary difference between a coach and a consultant is this: Consultants *tell*. They come to fix things and find solutions. Sometimes they're engaged for short, surgical strikes and sometimes they receive long-term assignments. Their work is often systems-based or operational.

Coaches *ask*. We come for the long haul to pose and wrestle with transformational questions and ideas that empower leaders to address and work through their challenges. Coaches involve the leaders fully in the heavy-lifting of solving their own problems, creating an increasingly skilled and independent leader. If we simply solved the problems of leadership for them, they would be back each week with a similar one, expecting us to solve it.

As coaches, we do bring our own experiences to leaders by seeing around corners and anticipating consequences or moves, like a chess game. We use our experience to push their thinking, to challenge them, provide resources, or help them plan professional development workshops, work with boards, prepare for or debrief an authentic conversation, and so on. Regardless of what the leader brings, we coach them to develop robust decision-making skills, to be self-aware, to learn how to treat others as they want to be treated. We coach leaders to a bigger vision of themselves than they might have.

Consciously practicing States of Being, supported by the 7EQs, is often an uplifting experience, one in which the leader and the coach interdependently build their coaching relationship. With each coaching session, both coach and leader can learn something new about themselves, each other, and about leadership. Coaching is rigorous and demanding: it requires stamina and doesn't always go well. It can sometimes feel intimidating and demoralizing, and we have to have ways to recover quickly so that we don't become overwhelmed or bring that energy to the next leader's session. Coaching is hard work that requires intentional self-care: physically, emotionally, and spiritually. Coaching dwells on sacred ground as people trust us with stories they rarely have the luxury of offering to anyone else. They look to us to guide them through the challenging labyrinth of urgent school leadership.

I have to work hard to live and dance with measured abandon within this space and not fall off the cliff. It's a constant challenge. Meditation, dancing, poetry, practicing gratitude and love, and having trusted friends and a coach of my own all help bring me back from the edge.

Chapter 1

The Why: Discovering, Developing, and Teaching the States of Being

Come to the edge.
We might fall.
Come to the edge.
It's too high!
COME TO THE EDGE!
And they came,
and he pushed,
and they flew.

—Christopher Logue

Coming to the Edge

Early in my career, I had an epiphany in the middle of a coaching session that changed the trajectory of my work. The biweekly phone calls I was having with a young, emerging leader in an urban school had not been going well. I noticed that just before every one of our calls, I felt a certain low-level dread, the kind that begins in my belly, works its way to my respiratory system where my breathing becomes shallow, then settles in the muscles in my neck that get stiff and sore. I tried to understand what it was about. But I was baffled.

What I did understand was that our sessions quickly devolved into variations on the same theme: One week it was about helping a specific teacher improve; the following week it was about helping another teacher improve, and so on. And we kept circling back to the same solutions and techniques we had talked about in previous coaching sessions. I felt annoyed. I found myself wondering why *she* couldn't make the connections from session to session, rather than why *I* couldn't see how I contributed to helping her stay stuck in this pattern. Ironically, I was trying to get her to see these teachers' strengths, without realizing that I was unable to see hers. Our pattern was getting very old, and I was starting to not like her very much, and sensed that she likely felt the same about me. This is a terrible feeling for a coach to have.

While I wasn't sure what role I played in the problem, I did know that if these coaching sessions weren't going well for me, they probably weren't going well for her either, and we were scheduled for another five months of working together. I took a deep breath and a bold leap of faith.

In advance of our next call, I decided to practice what I had been coaching her to do—begin with self to prepare for authentic conversations. This is a three-part breathing and centering exercise. Step one: I inhale four counts then exhale eight counts to reduce the emotional response in my amygdala and to reset my prefrontal cortex. In other words, to calm down. Step two: Silently notice and name my feelings—frustration and dread—because unacknowledged feelings can eclipse thinking. Step three: Smile in recognition of the familiar feeling because genuine smiling (the Duchenne smile), and feeling the smile, releases mood-enhancing endorphin hormones and the stress-reducing cortisol, adrenaline, and dopamine hormones. The Duchenne smile also lowers my blood pressure.

The second thing I practice is a self query: What transformational end do I have in mind? In this instance, it's to understand the role I'm playing in the discomfort of our calls in order to change them. Because I *appreciate that everyone has a piece of the truth,* I see that I need to *gather perspectives,* then engage her in solving the problem.

I began our next call with, "I've been noticing that our calls don't seem to be going very well. It seems that we talk about the same issues, most of the time around teacher performance, and go over the same material each time. The impact is that I don't feel very effective as your coach and am not enjoying our calls. I'm wondering how these calls are going for you."

I could hear her take a deep breath followed by silence, then a sigh. "I don't like our calls very much either and don't look forward to them." While my ego felt bruised initially, I also felt a deep sense of relief. Maybe now we could figure this out together. I said, "I am so relieved to hear you say this, and I'm hoping that we can figure out what's going on and how to improve our calls. Can you tell me more about what's going on for you?"

And then came the revelation she offered: "I feel like I have to have a problem each time we talk so I, well, I make one up."

I discovered that in my efforts to try to ameliorate her initial strong sense of deficits, I had in fact succumbed to her need to dwell in them.

How did I make this happen? What was I doing? Practicing *Be Curious,* I discovered that I took her down a path of deficits and never found my/our way back to her highest self—her assets—the very thing I was committed to doing as a coach. And if I was doing this with her, was I also doing this with other leaders? I felt at once mortified and hopeful. Everyone is my teacher. Everyone is my teacher. Everyone is my teacher kept echoing in my head like a mantra trying to rescue me.

She went on to tell me that when I started each call by asking, "What's on your plate today?," she interpreted that as needing to have a problem. Because I always tried to help her solve the problem she presented, she thought she was on the right track. Worse yet, I was forcing her to have deficits that she may not have had. She also said that I often sounded annoyed with her. She might as well have punched me in the stomach for how that made me feel. Here I was, a woman who prided herself on being so attuned to coaching to leaders' highest selves, when, in fact, I was coaching to this leader's deficits. She also offered that it took her a little while to "recover" from our calls each time. She admitted that this was a very scary thing to be telling me as her coach. I responded that I was extremely grateful for her truthfulness and apologized profusely for putting her in this position week after week.

I was pretty devastated by her analysis. But I took another deep breath and said that I would like to hit the reset button and begin all over with her if she would agree to do this. She was a bit tentative, yet to her credit and generosity of spirit, she said yes.

It was in that moment that I realized I needed a new approach— a new way to begin each coaching session to replace my standard "What's on your plate today?," because this question bypasses strengths and easily elicits deficits-based responses. It's no wonder. Many urgent school leaders begin as teachers who work their way through the pipeline. As the late educator and pedagogy scholar Martin Haberman often reminded us in his work, teachers never think they're good enough and tend to carry this mindset with them into leadership, and the cycle continues, even when they think they're coaching others to assets. This is evidenced by a commonly accepted practice of offering deficits-based comments to a teacher or other staff member sandwiched in between positive comments. It might go something like this:

> During my observation today, I noticed that your students were much more engaged. Good job. I didn't, however, hear them answering questions that demonstrate critical thinking. Work on that for our next observation. I did notice that you have been working on getting students to leave the classroom in an orderly manner. Good work.

This kind of coaching is anchored in the notion that, as long as we also offer praise, it will help the teacher improve if we point things out that work, don't work, or need more work. In fact, it deflates them. It's hard to hear compliments when they're punctuated by criticism, even soft criticism that translates to and reinforces their fear: You're not good enough.

In addition, as I researched and observed, I also became increasingly aware that while some strengths-based coaching might have been occurring, there was not a structured way to translate these strengths to areas of development. It was also more common to find results-oriented, transactional-based, fix-the-problem coaching rather than transformational coaching—the kind that takes the long view of development and teaches the leader to learn to solve her own problems by calling on her strengths.

I decided to investigate how one of my own early mentors inspired me to learn from my successes. My dance teacher Mario Melodia taught me how to do a triple pirouette by *coaching to my assets* and *imbuing me with my own intelligence*. He asked me to notice what I was doing right in performing single and double turns: I planted my feet, found a focal point, relaxed, breathed, and visualized myself completing a successful pirouette. When I applied these techniques to the triple pirouette, with a little extra coaching from him about momentum, I was able to perfect it. He also taught me how to rise to the challenging demands of performance by helping me notice what I did well in rehearsal, including concentration, repetition, focus, and belief in myself. I learned how to transfer these strengths to other areas of my life as well.

He also *boldly told the truth* because he thought it was ethical and kind to tell students when they weren't rising to their level of excellence. He could do this because he built trust by *teaching to our highest selves*. He fostered our self-esteem, not by telling us that everything we did was wonderful, but by setting extremely high expectations and helping us meet them. When a student struggled, he came to her side, took her hand, and slowly taught her the step(s) until she learned them while we watched or practiced to deepen our own experience. Then, we all did the sequence together so he could check for understanding, praising the student who had previously struggled as we traveled across the room. "You all have the steps. Now, make it your own." And we did.

Another important mentor who informed the development of my coaching practice was Peg Rogers, my first female mentor/boss. She taught me the importance of asking questions anchored in the intention of helping people *see and become their highest selves*, as she consistently did with me, a practice that became the cornerstone of my coaching work. She expected excellence and taught it by example. She protected her staff when we were under fire. She let us see her mistakes, make our own, and taught me about forgiveness and humility. "I'll let you go to the edge, but I won't let you fall off." She fostered my creativity, encouraged me to take risks, and asked me what my dreams were—the thwarted and the still unrealized. She taught me how to build and nurture a team and to organize a community dedicated to dismantling racism. She pushed me to examine my assumptions, biases, responses, and interactions within the community. She taught me that urgency and humanity can coexist.

Perhaps, most important, Peg *listened to my stories*, helping me discover myself through them. Learning to *listen with presence and purpose* became a skill I honed and expanded over the years from individuals to groups: Stories help us understand ourselves, and each other. I believe that stories are the entry point to transformational change.

I knew I was fortunate to have these two life-shaping models, and I set out to find a way to translate the success of their approaches into my own leadership coaching. This led to the formulation of a new opening query with the leader whose coaching sessions weren't going well because they kept her stranded in her deficits. After much thought and tinkering, I landed on "Tell me about a success, big or small, you recently had," followed by, "What did you do to make that happen?" From that day forward, we took a new path, and we later agreed that we both looked forward to these calls by being bold, compassionate, and honest.

After that session, my coaching practice began to move in a new and more productive direction. I began to deconstruct what I was doing when I was coaching, then codify it. I began to step outside of myself and "listen in" on my own calls in an effort to create a methodology of coaching. In addition to the follow-up notes I made for leaders, I made notes to myself during and after calls, then recorded coaching calls, with the leader's permission.

As part of the process, I began to pay close attention to what was occurring within me as I listened to leaders unfold stories, noticing how this influenced my responses. I paid attention to my thoughts, feelings, triggers, breathing, respiration, and the course corrections this noticing informed. I learned to sense more quickly when my compassion began to collapse into judgment, to feel when my curiosity was being undermined by impatience or ego, and when I was reflexively slipping into consulting—telling the leader what to do instead of helping them discover their own answers. Perhaps, most important, I discovered what I was doing that was working so that I could repeat it.

This was the beginning of the States of Being that evolved over time as I listened as my own witness to the coaching sessions I engaged in. I became more comfortable with and confident in the practice, because leaders reported that our coaching sessions were helping them become more effective by seeing teachers improve.

As I listened to the stories leaders told me when describing their own coaching styles, I discovered two related things: (1) they lived with the premise that they had to have all the answers; and (2) they were driven by the need to see test scores improve. The combination of this assumption with a results-based imperative translated into leaders simply telling staff what to do. And they couldn't figure out why they weren't seeing progress. Observations like these helped me understand the importance of *listening* and *being curious* about what was already working and figuring out how to leverage that. It also effectively demonstrated, how attachment to outcomes—test scores—rather than process, was the enemy of progress.

One of the most challenging aspects for leaders is, "How can I get him to improve if I don't tell him what he's doing wrong? But something shifts for nearly every leader once they begin to practice looking and listening for successful moments, capturing what the teacher did to make them happen, and coaching the teacher to leverage these strengths to address areas of development. Over time, they have a moment of clarity, much like my own aha moment described above. Plus, there is a surprising benefit: we feel better when we connect from our highest selves to others' highest selves.

Eventually, I created a coaching pilot program for the KIPP

Foundation where I began to introduce States of Being. The nine coaches and about a dozen leaders reported feeling much better about themselves because most people don't like telling people what they're doing wrong. Once we were all using the States of Being, I noticed I became more authentic with leaders. I was more transparent about what might be happening to me, and let them know which State of Being I was using. I felt more at ease letting them peek behind the curtain. They reported that it was helpful for them to hear that I still struggle and make mistakes, and were eager to enhance their mastery of the States of Being as a set of tools they could use.

Although the work of equity had always been integrated into my work as an educator, community organizer, journalist, artist, activist, and coach, the evolution of the 7EQs came a few years after the States of Being. It became clear that equity issues were not being addressed with intentionality in most schools, or by most of the 40 coaches I was now working with. I challenged myself to codify a way to infuse equity into coaching by continuing the ongoing research I have engaged in since 1968, by gathering major thinkers and practitioners in the field, and by doing a lot of listening. It took about a year to form the 7EQs.

As a part of this process, I asked nearly 20 coaches who had been working with me for about a decade, to join me in this dangerous work. "Dangerous" because they would have to commit, as I did, to exploring their own biases—explicit and unconscious. To their credit, they signed on. This required a new kind of risk and boldness for all of us as we challenged ourselves and each other, naming moments that felt biased or racist, sometimes sinking into dark places, listening to each other's stories and fears, and sometimes just sitting in silence together while we absorbed what was happening. Our vision was that our personal and collective work would influence their willingness to *be bold* in their own schools and with the leaders they coached, who in turn would take the bold steps to address equity issues head-on in their schools.

By the time I handed the reins of the leadership coaching program to Pam Moeller in 2016, the States of Being, supported by the 7EQs, had become a deeply rooted, shared coaching language and practice by the roughly 40 coaches and the several hundred sitting principals and emerging leaders that they coach. The cascading effect through teachers to students is the manifestation of my dream.

I have come to understand that there are other intangibles embedded in effective leadership coaching that guide me, like those described by legendary NBA basketball coach Phil Jackson in *Eleven Rings*:

> I can't pretend to be an expert in leadership theory. But what I do know is that the art of transforming a group of young, ambitious individuals into an integrated championship team is not a mechanistic process. It's a mysterious juggling act that requires not only a thorough knowledge of the time-honored laws of the game but also an open heart, a clear mind, and the deep curiosity about the ways of the human spirit.

Julian's Story: 2011

A school leader we'll call "Julian" tells me that a math teacher he coaches has good lesson plans, but he can't get the teacher to improve his instruction. The more Julian describes his work with this teacher, the more worked up he gets, punctuated by: "He doesn't do what I tell him!"

I notice Julian's frustration and want to make sure not to deepen it. I realize that to help him solve this problem, I have to help him access his thinking rather than stay stranded in his feelings. And, I need more data to guide us. So, I ask: "Can you tell me more about how you have been coaching the teacher?"

With astonishing candor, Julian replies: "I coach by offering a shit sandwich." Translation: a negative statement slipped between two chunks of positive news, then telling the teacher what to do.

Julian continues: "I give him good things to do in the classroom." Bewildered, Julian wonders aloud why the teacher's instruction never improves. I could tell Julian why, and tell him what to do differently. But adults don't change their behavior when told what to do—like his teacher. In fact, this approach generally does just the opposite. It tends to make people feel dispirited and fold up. What's more, trust erodes, relationships collapse, people feel bad about themselves, and they begin to shut down or look for other work. Adults and children need to participate in the discovery, to feel creative, seen, and honored.

I choose to coach Julian toward his own discovery, and in the process, hope to offer him a model for coaching his math teacher.

"Is he good at anything?" I ask. Suddenly, Julian becomes positively animated: "YES! He's great with relationships." I ask him to tell me *how* he's good at relationships. Julian easily breaks it down into documentable components: "He talks to students, checks in with them, comes back around, and checks in again to see how they're doing. He helps them solve problems and make good decisions. And he celebrates them when they do the right thing." It's impressive how well Julian knows this teacher: It's clear he has been observing him in the classroom beyond instruction—he sees his humanity. I let Julian know this then respond: "That sounds like some of the elements for implementing a lesson plan—check to see what students know, teach, check for understanding, check in again, guide them toward problem solving and toward discovering the right answers, then celebrate them when they get the answer. What if you take the teacher through this same process and guide him to translating his skills at relationship-building to implementing a lesson?"

Julian enthusiastically endorses this idea; he immediately makes connections and talks about ways he could do this. He expresses amazement at how simple this transformation seems to be, that he can use the teacher's strengths to help him with his areas of development. Then he falls silent. Julian is now leaning forward, his hands clasped, his arms resting on his thighs, his head shifting back and forth between gazing at the floor in contemplation and looking up at me.

We sit in a brief silence together. He seems simultaneously lit up and demoralized. Lit up because he has just learned something new and recognizes there is another way. He says that *coaching to assets* feels more congruent with his own good nature, that bringing out the best in others feels like it will bring out the best in himself as well: "I don't like telling teachers what they're doing wrong and telling them what to do," he says confessionally. "I just didn't know how else to do it." Julian is also demoralized, and a little angry, as he reveals he has just fired the teacher and wishes he would have tried coaching to the teacher's strengths. We sit in a new, soft silence evoked by Julian's revelation. As I would come to discover in my coaching, pieces of songs and poetry often flood my unconscious to inform me. This time, in that silence, it was the last few lines of Marge Piercy's poem "A Just Anger":

> A good anger acted upon
> is beautiful as lightning
> and swift with power.
> A good anger swallowed,
> clots the blood
> to slime.

Weaving States of Being and 7EQs into Julian's Story

Note: In this section, the language of both the States of Being and the 7EQs I engaged in with Julian are italicized as a way of introducing some of them and demonstrating how to weave them.

The coaching session I describe above was the very first one I had with Julian. It arose spontaneously out of a professional development (PD) I was offering for a small group of school and district leaders from across the country that I was considering hiring as coaches. At the outset, I introduced the concept of coaching to assets. Seated across the table from me is Julian, a tall, African-American man in his late 20s or early 30s, leaning back in his chair, arms folded across his chest, a strong jaw, head slightly cocked, looking at me with a piercing gaze that seems to be saying, How do I know I can trust you? Or your States of Being? Prove yourself. (Over time, he would come to discover that this mistrust was born out of resentment of being bombarded by his experience with many white leaders who were inauthentic in their desire to address equity.)

I practice *Quiet the Ego* by *checking in with myself before checking out* with Julian, and sense in myself what I imagine his teachers might feel in his presence. I notice that I could easily feel intimidated by his physical stature, chiseled features, and authoritative voice and questioning eyes, if I weren't confident in States of Being. If I didn't have experience to call on. If I didn't have a sense of why I am here in this moment. There's something else. *I begin with self to examine implicit and explicit biases.* Would I experience this moment differently if one of the white men in the room assumed Julian's posture? One of the white women? Then, I stop to consider how to continue to *create a sense of belonging.* To *create conditions for Julian to continue to feel free to be authentic.* I wonder how he sees me (a small, older, white Jewish woman), returning his direct gaze. Regardless of how much work I have done examining my own biases, I am aware that it's an ongoing process to confront the internalized messages I received growing up about the threatening nature of Black men.

I take a quiet breath and go to work, zeroing in on his earnest concern that he expressed during the impromptu coaching session I offered him to demonstrate how it works: "I don't get how I can coach to strengths." I want to *imbue Julian with his own intelligence,* and *help him connect the dots.* I need more data to know how to do that, so I begin by *being curious* when I ask him to tell me more about how he coaches his teacher. I'm gathering data to learn what he already knows, what he does well, what might be missing, and where this might lead me/us. I *honor Julian's Story.* When I hear him describe the "shit sandwich," coaching to deficits, and telling the teacher what to do, wrapped inside a strong sense of frustration, I could allow myself to get mired in the "shit" and feel judgment toward Julian for taking this approach. I notice this thought and feeling, understanding that I have a choice in how to respond. I choose, instead, to *see Julian's highest self*—the one who wants to help his teacher get better but doesn't know how to make that happen. I *ask a nonjudgmental question,* looking for strengths that Julian is able to identify in his math teacher: "Is the teacher good at anything?" By *imbuing Julian with his own intelligence,* the questions can *guide him to his own discovery,* and he easily and enthusiastically runs off a list of his math teacher's relationship strengths. By acknowledging to Julian that it's impressive how well he knows his teacher, I am also *coaching to Julian's strengths* and building trust.

When Julian tells me his math teacher is good at relationships— this is the *What* that I'm looking for. It is impressive that Julian knows this and hasn't been blinded to the teacher's strengths by his inability to help the teacher improve. Next, in order to help Julian learn how to translate strengths to transform areas of development—the fundamental purpose of coaching to assets—I ask him to describe *how* the teacher is good at building relationships. This is the key to the connection. When I help Julian make that connection, he has a revelation alongside his sense of defeat with the math teacher. I silently recognize this as a deep learning moment.

Before we end our impromptu session, I ask him if he would like a follow-up session. He says yes, then asks if I would consider being his coach moving forward. I agree to this and feel a sense of relief and gratitude for this unselfish man, for his deep commitment to the children and the teachers in his school, and for his desire to *become his highest self.* I also feel gratitude for the gift of this session and for Julian's willingness to make himself so vulnerable—a quality, I will learn over our coaching sessions, that is difficult for him. I am so humbled by and grateful for his developing trust. I thank him.

Chapter 2

See the Higher Self
Coach to Assets

This [coaching to assets] helped me to continuously look at my strengths, and with confidence, build the framework of how to apply those strengths regardless of the pending task, project, or conversation. Sustainability in my job comes primarily from effectively managing the stress connected with my job responsibilities (supporting principals). Through my experiences being coached, and coaching others, I've more consistently abandoned a deficits-mindset in myself and my direct reports. Those who I supervise (who are mostly coaches themselves) have begun to adopt many of my new habits related to building strength-based frameworks. This is proof-positive for me that I'm building capacity, and thus becoming a more effective leader and leadership developer.

—Julian (one year after we
began working together)

LEARNING FROM OUR FAILURES CAN be useful. But identifying what we're doing wrong only tells us what not to do again and does little to help us understand what we're doing right so we can continue to do it. By focusing on what we do well (perhaps intuitively or instinctively), we learn to exercise our strengths intentionally, and strategically. Coaching to leaders' assets, strengths, and talents provides them with information about what they already know how to do, and hones their ability to use their assets in other situations. When we coach to people's strengths, we build loyalty and trust, which makes it possible for us to *Be Bold* when we need to be.

Unless we can truly *see the higher self* in others (and in ourselves), and anchor our coaching sessions in successes and strengths, we will fall into the seductive trap of defining our leaders by what we and they come to believe are their weaknesses, as I did with the leader who guided me to the epiphanous moment I described in the prelude. We and they will view them as "less than," at best, and "broken," at worst—and we will be in a constant state of trying to fix them. We will have no image of them flying, only flailing or failing. Teachers need to sense themselves succeeding if we want to keep them on the job long enough to build mastery and institutional memory, two critical links to countering student attrition and the opportunity gap in schools that serve primarily children of color. Coaching to assets offers collaborative access to what leaders bring to their work, what they excel in, and what their dreams are. We coach leaders to infuse their community with its aspirational vision of serving students.

Coaching to Assets

Imagine the urgent school leader waking up every morning with the fierce desire to make a difference in her students' lives through the staff she leads and supervises. Imagine her as a teacher with a challenging student she successfully mentored before she became a leader.

You learn of this success through a story she shares when you practice *being curious*. Imagination is a key characteristic of effective coaches. By engaging our own imaginations, we help the leader tap into her creativity, an essential hallmark of successful leaders and a key to wanting to stay on the job.

As coaches, we imagine the leader at her best, regularly see the promise in her—her highest self. We *imbue the leader or teacher with her own intelligence* and *help her connect the dots* from previous successful experiences she has had, especially with those new to teaching or leading. Perhaps her experiences might have been as a member of an affinity organization, a sports team, or any other group she has led. These successes and strengths can be translated to her current work using the *See the Higher Self* State of Being.

It takes everything we can muster *not* to put our attention on the things that aren't working, but it's a discipline that must be practiced in order to be successful. This isn't to say that the leader shouldn't notice areas where the teacher needs further development; it means that we coach the leader to notice what the teacher does well so that the teacher can call upon these strengths in other areas of development. As coaches, we want to model this practice and be transparent about it so that our leaders can learn how to do this with the people they supervise and coach.

Rituals are also important. I begin each coaching session with an opening ritual to set a listening tone. It's also a way to be fully *present* to each other. This helps the leader step out of her fast-paced busy day, stop, and make space for the session. Being intentionally present helps build trust. You can establish a ritual that works for you. I begin by asking the leader to join me in a four-count inhale and eight-count exhale, to share the process of being *present* together, and to offer her the opportunity to reset her frontal cortex. I then ask her to notice herself, to note where she might be holding tension. We repeat the breathing. Then, for the third round, I ask her to set an intention for the session. I ask her to inhale what she needs more of, and to exhale what she would like to impart to her community. It's amazing how often leaders want to inhale and exhale variations on the theme of Peace/Love, Calm/Joy, Relaxed/Focus. Breathing these intentions with them helps me sync up with them and also helps center me.[1]

Leaders often tell me how much they've come to depend on breathing, especially because they feel like they're drinking from the firehose most of the time. Within a few inhales and exhales, I can hear their voices deepen in tone, see their faces relax, and observe their rhythm slowing down.

After our opening ritual, we begin with the very first *coaching-to-assets* question: What success, big or small, have you recently had? Or, we narrow the frame by asking the leader what success, big or small she has had recently in a particular area of development. For example, What success, big or small, have you recently had in creating a sense of belonging? Or, interrupting racism? Having an authentic conversation with a staff member? And so on.

Then we mine the How to capture her strengths: What did you do to make that happen? As the leader tells her story, the coach creates a list of present (imperative) tense verbs/phrases, associated States of Being, and/or any of the 7EQs that the leader used to create the success. We capture the verbs in present tense because they

---

1. It's worth noting that school leaders who have integrated intentional breathing into their own lives, are also practicing it with their students. Here is what one emerging leader wrote to me: "Today, Kyle [student] wanted us to breathe in the word *trustworthiness*. Oh, Linda! So amazing! During a class, two students were starting to have a tiff. I reminded one student to let it go, and he said, 'Ms. G., I don't understand how you can let it go.' Then another student, David, who had come to a breathing and refocusing practice, said, 'Ms. G., he should come to our breathing class!' That was followed by a chorus of 'What?!' and 'I wanna go!' This small flame of interest is turning into a blaze of glory! Tomorrow, with Kyle, Ke'Andre, and David, I'm going to start to map out a proposal for the principal suggesting that we share our [breathing and refocusing] techniques at a staff PD."

are dynamic strengths that can always be accessed. These strengths will then be tapped to address a challenge the leader presents. And leaders *always* have challenges: hiring issues, board issues, coaching new teachers, failing students, an angry parent, a student who brings a gun to school, a flawed policy, a teacher who suddenly quits. A student who dies.

A common challenge for inexperienced teachers is classroom engagement—what is often referred to as classroom management. This becomes challenging for those who coach/supervise the teacher as well, because they become fixated on the times he isn't responsive to his students, or the students are not responsive to the teacher. Our job is to help focus the leader's attention on times when these things *are* occurring, when the students are engaged, alert, involved, and learning. Even if it's only once during the observation. It is in these moments the leader will help the teacher discover what he is doing when he is engaging students so that he can actively employ these techniques routinely.

Several things will emerge from this process. The leader will build a trusting relationship with the teacher, an essential element in coaching him to teach well and thrive. Trust, in turn, opens the door for the leader to offer suggestions that the teacher will be more likely to add to his toolbox. Trust also helps normalize the awkwardness of the teacher and leader practicing these tools together as if they are in the classroom. The teacher will learn to notice what he's doing when he is being successful so he can repeat it with intention. And, the leader/coach can begin to discipline himself to notice other areas of strength this teacher has and expand them, transform them, and continue to *imbue him with his own intelligence.*

We coach the leader to the higher self with a cascading end in mind: The process will be infused throughout the school community, from leader to managers, to teachers, to staff, and ultimately, to students. The hope is that *seeing the higher self* will become an instrument for living—a way of life. A coaching culture.

A Meditation on *See the Higher Self*

An emerging leader we'll call Sonya unfolds a story about a successful experience she had coaching a struggling teacher, shifting from the deficits model to assets. She had previously focused her classroom observations on the teacher's areas of struggle, pointing them out to her during their one-on-one coaching sessions: "You didn't have control of your classroom"; "You didn't check for understanding"; "You didn't move around the room enough," and so on. She gave the teacher instructions on what she wanted her to do to remedy all of these areas. Sonya couldn't figure out why the teacher's performance, and student data, didn't improve. "I told her what to do," she tells me in a frustrated tone. "I couldn't figure out why she didn't get any better. I felt so frustrated. And so did she. Her morale began to take a real dive."

Sonya decided to try *coaching to the teacher's assets* instead, drawing on our success model that we begin each of our sessions with. She disciplined herself to notice what the teacher did well during her observation, not the myriad areas that could use improvement. She noted to me how challenging it is to do this. I let her know that I have to discipline myself to do this as well and assured her that focusing on strengths doesn't preclude noticing areas of development as well. It means moving the strengths to the foreground as a way of addressing development.

Sonya was amazed by what she noticed when she focused on what the teacher was doing well during a successful lesson, strengths that had previously been eclipsed by focusing on her deficits. She described how the teacher used culturally relevant material. She also noted that she instinctively planted her feet when she asked students thought-provoking questions. She gave them time to think before asking them to respond. When a student offered a thoughtful, critical response, the teacher went beyond saying "Good," or "Well done." She demonstrated how to ask thoughtful, nonjudgmental questions that continued to push the student's thinking, then invited others in the class to respond to the student's higher self as well by *being curious, asking nonjudgmental questions*. As the students engaged, the teacher translated their responses into elements of what critical thinking is and wrote them on the board to provide visual reinforcement.

During Sonya's next one-on-one coaching session with the teacher, she offered her observations about what she saw her do well. Then, using the State of Being *Be Curious*, Sonya asked the teacher if she could identify what made this lesson so strong. The teacher said that she spent more time planning the lesson because she was teaching an essay that had cultural relevance to her and to the students. This kept them engaged. She visualized herself teaching, including moving around the room, and imagining herself waiting for students to respond. She planned questions to pose, and practiced reading the material out loud for dramatic effect. She even practiced smiling in the mirror. At the end of the one-on-one coaching session, the teacher said she felt grateful for learning what she was doing well. She also admitted that she felt excited about teaching the next day, rather than worried, as she usually did.

While it may not be possible to teach culturally relevant material all the time, the success and strengths that the teacher discovered through the coaching process will help inspire her to call on them in other lessons. Consequently, her students will stay inspired and engaged, and their performance will improve. Education researcher Susan Moore Johnson has shown that when students—particularly underserved students—do well, teachers are more likely to feel good about their work and stay on the job longer. The longer they stay on the job, the more confident, expert, and creative their teaching becomes, the more students they influence, and the school's culture becomes one of dynamic teaching and learning. And the longer teachers stay on the job, the longer students tend to do well in school.

As Sonya told her story, I wrote down the strengths that she used with the teacher (drawn from the States of Being and the 7EQs) in the present-imperative tense ("see the higher self") as opposed to the past tense ("she saw the higher self") so that the list of strengths would become living tools for her to use again. Here is how I captured what I heard.

Success: I shifted my perspective on observing a teacher and changed the way I coached her. This resulted in beginning to build a trusting relationship with her and seeing her excited to teach for the first time.

Strengths: What did you do to make this happen?

- See the Higher Self (Coach to Assets)
- Be Curious (Ask Nonjudgmental Questions)
- Honor Story (Listen)
- Be Present (Remain Unattached to Outcome)
- Imbue Others with Their Own Intelligence (Help Them Connect the Dots)
- Create a sense of belonging
- Create conditions for staff and students to feel free to be authentic

Part of the process of recording strengths is to read each one back to the leader and ask, "Do you understand how I heard this?" This practice offers data about what the leader knows about herself, ensures that she and I are understanding her strengths the same way, introduces new information about the leader, and illuminates blind spots—hers and mine. Sonya understood that she *remained unattached to outcome* by not worrying about data but, instead, focused on how the teacher was teaching. She wondered how I derived "create a sense of belonging." I responded that she acknowledged that the teacher was using material that was culturally relevant to her and to her students. Sonya also wondered how I heard "create conditions for staff and students to feel free to be authentic." *Imbuing her with her own intelligence*, I asked Sonya how she felt when I *coached to her assets*. She replied: I feel seen. Oh, and free to be myself without worry that you'll tell me how I'm failing.

Sonya did a good job shifting her perspective. I asked her if she felt ready to use the *See the Higher Self (Coach to Assets)* model next time. She said yes. She would ask the teacher to define her successes rather than define them for her, because people trust, integrate, and internalize their strengths by discovering and naming them, not by simply being told they have them.

Leveraging Strengths to Address a Challenge

One of the big benefits of *coaching to assets* is that as soon as we begin to identify strengths, they can be leveraged across unrelated situations. For example, I asked Sonya what challenge she wanted to address.

Her first response was, "I want to get this teacher to stop being negative at staff meetings." Identifying a behavior she wanted to see this teacher stop, rather than a transformative behavior she wanted the teacher to practice, is a common response when leaders and coaches haven't yet internalized the States of Being process. I responded: "One of the things we've learned from neuroscience, and from meditation, is that the brain needs something to work toward rather than against." *Being curious* and *imbuing Sonya with her own intelligence*, I ask her what a positive interaction at staff meetings might look like for this teacher. I waited through her silence. Then she said: "That's really hard. I don't know."

I followed with the question that often elicits a knowing response: "If you did know, what would you say?" She quickly responded: "I would like her to listen to other points of view more. To contribute more." There it was: she had identified behaviors the teacher could adopt, rather than behaviors she should cease. Here's how I used *Be Curious (Ask Nonjudgmental Questions)* to gather more data:

> LB: It sounds as if you know that she has valuable things to contribute. What might those be?
>
> SONYA: Hmmm...I have to think about it. I feel so negative toward her.
>
> LB: Can you think of a time you saw her being positive when she was teaching?
>
> (Sonya gets silent here again. I can see that she's beginning to feel bad as her spine rounds into the back of the chair. She acknowledges that she is seeing a pattern in herself that she doesn't like.)
>
> SONYA: Wow! I put people in boxes pretty quickly.
>
> LB: (Nonjudgmental question to gather data) Is this new to you?
>
> SONYA: No. I realize that I do it a lot. (She gets teary.)

Earlier, in the Prelude, I noted that coaching isn't for everyone. That it takes emotional stamina. We have to *be present* to the emotions of others, not deny them by trying to fix them or interrupt them. When unexamined feelings or situations get stimulated, they are often accompanied by crying, or silence. Sometimes by fast, non-stop talking. Sometimes by shaking or sweating. Even laughter. My intention is not to try to make Sonya feel better, or fix things, which would deny her feelings. It is to move her toward identifying and solving the challenge.

In these moments, it's essential that we *check in before checking out.* I need to understand how I'm feeling as Sonya explores this emotional space. This is where we have to be crystal clear where the space between coach and therapist is. I'm very clear that I don't want to mine Sonya's past or strand her in her feelings. The antidote is to bring her back into her strong thinking.

> LB: (I wait a few beats until she seems present again. She dabs her eyes, takes a breath, and adjusts her body to listening mode. She shifts in the chair and gets eye contact.)
>
> LB: (Quietly) Sometimes people cry in coaching sessions.
>
> SONYA (Laughs)
>
> LB: Do you feel ready to continue?
>
> SONYA: Yes.
>
> LB: (Offering information on the State of Being *Interrupt Patterns [Notice Repetition]*) We all have patterns. We often develop them as part of our family dynamic or situations that have occurred. You might have an understanding of how your pattern evolved. It's only important that *you* understand this. What's important for our work together is that you recognize the pattern and want to interrupt it so it doesn't interfere with your leadership. (See Chapter 8.)
>
> SONYA: I do. I know where it comes from.
>
> LB: (I repeat) It's not important that I know the origin. It's only important that you know.

(*Note*: People usually understand where their patterns originated. Sometimes, a leader tells the origin of the pattern. If they do, our job is to receive it, acknowledge it, without furthering it.)

LB: We interrupt our patterns by recognizing and replacing the behavior. For example: We'll have a better chance of giving up cigarettes if we eat carrots. Or something else to chew on. Would you like to interrupt the pattern you describe: putting people in boxes pretty quickly? (It's important to remind the leader of the discovered pattern to make sure we're on the same page.)

SONYA: Yes. I'd like to.

LB: Can you think of something to replace the box with?

SONYA: (Silence while thinking) I think I can see the box opened up and flat on the ground underneath her. Like a square platform she's standing on.

LB: What a clear image. Now that we know we have to have something to work toward rather than against, and you have an image of the teacher standing on a square ground, with no barriers, can you imagine her succeeding at a staff meeting?

SONYA: (Now sitting with a longer spine and leaning forward into our conversation. She responds animatedly.) Yes. First, I have to see her enter the meeting in this new light that I have on her. I can see her entering with a pleasant demeanor instead of looking unhappy to be there.

LB: Which discovered strengths can you call on? (I show her the list.)

- See the Higher Self (Coach to Assets)

- Be Curious (Ask Nonjudgmental Questions)

- Honor Story (Listen)

- Be Present (Remain Unattached to Outcome)

- Imbue Others with Their Own Intelligence (Help Them Connect the Dots)

- Create a sense of belonging

- Create conditions for staff and students to feel free to be authentic

SONYA: I can *see her higher self.* I can commit to creating a sense of belonging for our diverse staff by *imbuing her with her own intelligence* and ask her in advance to present her approach to teaching culturally relevant material. I can offer resources. I think this help would create conditions for staff to feel free to be authentic. I can picture this happening.

LB: How do you think she will respond?

SONYA: Based on our recent coaching session, I think she'll feel good about it. Seen. Appreciated.

LB: This sounds very positive. You worked so hard in this coaching session. Thank you for your trust.

SONYA: Thank you.

This is the beginning of the dance for Sonya with this teacher. She will likely experience steps forward and backward. There are many influencing factors beyond the lives we see in our leaders, and those they see in their teachers. Our job as coaches is to hold the space for them, listen well, be consistent and nimble, and remind them and ourselves that progress is not a straight line.

Ending the Coaching Session

Closing rituals are as important as opening ones are. A question I have come to cherish is, "What's clearer to you now?" This helps me know what has been most salient for the leader, and helps her register what she's learned by saying it aloud. The answer is almost always transformational, rather than transactional. This is what we are coaching toward. I also ask the question occasionally throughout the session, as well, as a guide for me to see where the leader is, what she understands, and to show me how to help her reset. I also ask, "What's clearer to you now?" when I'm stuck. The leader's answer always guides me where to go next because *everyone has a piece of the truth*. Another closing question option is, "What leadership lesson have you learned today?" Let your intuition guide you toward the question that seems right.

Sonya responds to "What's clearer to you now?" with the following: "I believe in talking with teachers the way I like to be talked to *and* the way they would like to be talked to. I focused on getting her to be a better teacher rather than focusing on her test scores." She notes that getting to the How of the What was very useful for her as a leader/coach. It gave her practical tools to help drive the transformation she had been looking for. She also says, "I am beginning to see how *coaching to strengths* helps collapse boxes and that I have work to do *interrupting my pattern*. How strengths are transferable from situation to situation." And finally, a common response: "I feel *so* much better coaching this way."

Sonya later reported that student scores in the teacher's class have been improving, and her trust with the teacher is deepening. The teacher's presentation at the meeting on teaching culturally relevant material opened up an important equity conversation that they have never had because it wasn't on Sonya's radar. Her newfound success helps her *be bolder* with the teacher as she continues to tackle each area that needs development, one at a time. And, Sonya has begun to more intentionally examine what an equitable school looks like. She notes that it is fraught with challenges. I send resources to her including an interview I did with educator and pedagogical theorist Gloria Ladson-Billings on the topic.

Helping leaders deconstruct their successes helps them know how to coach their teachers more effectively, elevates their own self-esteem, and gives them energy to do the hard work of urgent school leadership.

COACHING MODEL

WHAT: See the Higher Self

WHY: Coaching to strengths identifies what we already know how to do well so we can continue doing it and can learn to use these strengths in other situations. When positive emotions are aroused, we are more open to new ideas and learning. Supervising and coaching to strengths builds trust, boosts engagement and loyalty, and leads to faster development for the person we are coaching. When we coach to assets and strengths, we initiate a cascading effect from leader to teachers to staff to students in order to create a coaching and teaching culture.

HOW: Coach to Assets
Begin with Self

Before your session:
- Imagine the person at moments when you saw or heard her succeeding.
- Inhale *listen* / exhale *compassion*.
- Throughout the session, notice your own feelings and silently name them in order to manage them. Notice your breathing and other cues that indicate you might be feeling distracted, stressed, or triggered, so that you can quiet your ego and be present to the leader. Intentional breathing, shifting your position in your chair, and placing two feet on the floor can help you reset.

With Leader

During the session:
- If you are comfortable, inhale and exhale with the leader to reset the frontal cortex, focus, and be present.
- Intention setting: Ask the leader, "What do you need more of for yourself right now? What do you want to infuse your school community with?"
- Common Responses: Need more calm/peace. Want to infuse community with joy/confidence. (Coach the leader to offer

transformational responses rather than a to-do list.)

- If you are comfortable, inhale and exhale these responses with the leader. This helps you know what state of mind the leader is in, what her school needs, and helps the two of you sync up quickly.

In person: Notice unspoken cues and facial expressions. Listen to word choice, tone, pauses, and breathing. Adapt your own listening cues through easy eye contact and natural, responsive gestures and/or facial expressions.

By phone: Listen to word choice, tone, pauses, breathing, and other vocal sounds that you have learned about how the leader processes. Offer your own occasional responses to help the leaders know you are listening.

- Wait through silences to allow for processing time.
- Try not to interrupt unless the leader gets stuck in a pattern.

Note: This State can be done in about 20 minutes by devoting roughly 25 percent to identifying strengths, and 75 percent to leveraging the strengths toward solving a problem.

Ask Asset-Based Questions
- Ask: "What success, big or small, have you recently had?" Or, narrow the frame to an area of development. Example: "What went well in your staff meeting?" "What went well in the conversation you had with the struggling teacher?"
- Write down the success
- Ask: "What did you do to make this happen?"

Honor Story / Capture Strengths
As the leader tells her story, write active (not past tense) verbs and phrases that capture strengths contributing to the success (especially strengths that engage States of Being and 7EQs). Using the imperative tense makes these living, dynamic strengths that can be called on in any situation. The leader speaks in prose, we listen for and capture specifics.

Sample success: I ran a PD session on how to use culturally relevant materials in the classroom that was successfully implemented by the teachers.

Sample strengths:
- Communicate vision for the end in mind
- Solicit input and feedback
- Include teachers as PD presenters
- Offer resources
- Be curious
- Send follow-up notes and gratitude
- Plan backwards
- Gather feedback
- Honor learning styles
- Quiet the ego
- Practice

Imbue Her with Her Own Intelligence (Help Her Connect the Dots)
- Read each strength to the colleague and ask, "Do you under-stand how I heard this word or phrase?" This is to ensure that she understands your interpretation from story to strength, to offer you data on what she knows about herself, to learn more about her, and to ensure that you are on the same page.
- Add other strengths you might have heard.

Reset
- Ask: "What's clearer to you now?"

Shift to Address a Challenge
- Ask: "What's the challenge you want to focus on now?" Or: "Last time you said you wanted to focus part of today on [insert challenge]. Is that still where you want to focus? Is there anything else that would be more beneficial?"
- Listen to the story and be curious. Trust your intuition. Remain unattached to outcome. Quiet the ego.

Leverage and Imbue
- Ask the leader to make connections: "Which of these strengths can you leverage to address this challenge?"
- Show (or read) the list of strengths to the leader (and offer your knowledge of previous strengths you gleaned).
- Add your suggestions from the list if needed.

- Or, narrow the frame to the next area of development.
- Offer other resources or tools as needed.

Be Curious
- Ask: "What's clearer to you now?" This question can be woven throughout the coaching session to engage in ongoing synthesis, and to help guide you when you feel stuck.

Practice
- Engage in real-time practice using identified strengths for the challenge you have addressed. Example: Practice how she will introduce the next part of her vision to her staff.
- Make a note of follow-up or action steps.

Close
- Ask: "What's clearer to you now?" Or: "What leadership lesson have you learned today?"
- Inhale and exhale her opening intention.

Send Notes and Attach Resources

Weaving the States of Being
The steps in this model are the *science*. The *art* of coaching to assets is to weave other States of Being into the session so that leaders can get to the heart of their strengths and leverage them in a quick, efficient, purposeful way.

Supporting States of Being
- Honor Story (Listen)
- Be Curious (Ask Nonjudgmental Questions)
- Imbue Them with Their Own Intelligence (Help Them Connect the Dots)
- Be Present (Remain Unattached to Outcomes)
- Acknowledge Mystery (Trust Intuition)
- Quiet the Ego (Check In before Checking Out)

Potential Traps
- Spending too much time capturing strengths

- Making the strengths too specific to one situation
- Naming the leader's strengths for her
- Not noticing and/or not interrupting deficits-based language in the leader's description of success

Chapter 3
Honor Story
Listen

You have to be careful telling things.
Some ears are tunnels.
Your words will go in and get lost in the dark.
Some ears are flat pans like the miners used
looking for gold.

What you say will be washed out with the stones.
You look for a long time till you find the right ears.
Till then, there are birds and lamps to be spoken to,
a patient cloth rubbing shine in circles,
and the slow, gradually growing possibility
that when you find such ears
they already know.

—Naomi Shihab Nye

STORY IS LIKE A THIRD participant in coaching conversations. Story is what brings a situation to life, illuminates how the storyteller views the world or a particular moment. It provides animation, poignancy, and context to data they provide. Embedded in the stories they tell us are strengths they embody, fears and challenges they struggle with. Regardless of the success or dilemma the leader brings to the coaching session, story is the vehicle for conveying it. The role of the coach is to *be present* to the story so that the leader can make sense of their situation. How we *listen to story* is as important as the telling, because leaders need to feel that we understand and have a quick grasp on what they bring—that our ears already know.

We create space for leaders to be heard and, sometimes, talk their way to understanding. Whether the story is five sentences or a few minutes long, it contains information that can help guide us. Story is the way we listen to and capture essential elements of successes and strengths a leader has, decisions they need to make, and the challenges they need help addressing. Perhaps it's a rough situation or conversation they want to debrief, or one that they anticipate having. Or maybe they need a thought partner; or perhaps it's simply a way to let go of a situation that occupies their attention and energy. Focused *listening* with the heart, head, and intuition, helps build trust with the leader, an essential aspect of effective coaching.

When stories are told within small groups in conditions that feel safe and respectful, with the *intention to listen* for elements that strike a chord in us, they can significantly benefit the teller, the witness, and the community, often in long-lasting ways. When we tell our stories within this protected space, in the absence of judgment, the teller often feels a sense of relief, of feeling seen and heard—sometimes for the first time. He often feels unburdened, stress begins to dissolve, new pathways appear. Story stimulates compassion, liberating us from the perception of the Other. Story can transform a sense of alienation into a sense of belonging, strengthening the sense of community. (For more on facilitating group storytelling, see "Build

Teams through Story" and "Create a Sense of Belonging through Story" at lindabelans.com.)

Listening

When leaders share their stories within the confidential confines of coaching, and we *listen without judgment, agenda or prescription*, we establish trust which creates the space for leaders to feel authentic, creating a sense of belonging for and with them. We learn to *listen* for silences, sighs, repetition, word choices, shifts in rhythm, tone, energy, and gesture/posture.

Sometimes, when a leader offers a story, our intuition tells us that they sound distant or disconnected from it. When I experience this, I ask the leader to try to tell the story in the present tense to bring them closer to it. It's uncanny how many details, images, sounds, or events emerge through this process.

It takes patience, emotional stamina, silence, and internal stillness to give our full attention to *honoring story* in service to the leader's development. William Butler Yeats captures this concept beautifully in "Earth, Fire, and Water" from *The Celtic Twilight*: "We can make our minds so like still water that beings gather about us that they may see, it may be, their own images, and so live for a moment with a clearer, perhaps even with a fiercer life because of our quiet."

A Meditation on *Honor Story*

Julian, the leader with the "shit-sandwich" story, got right to the point: He couldn't get a teacher to improve his lesson implementation. This makes it easy to begin coaching Julian, because he comes to the session knowing that he wants to find a solution to a specific problem.

But sometimes a coaching session can feel like John Cage's composition "Indeterminacy," a series of random, unrelated story snippets strung together. At first, I track to *listen* to where these stories might be going. After a few minutes, I begin to realize that they don't seem to be going anywhere, that they have no apparent connection to each other. *Checking in before checking out*, I realize I am on high alert, *listening* for a thread. Sometimes, depending on how many coaching sessions I've had that day, I can even feel impatient. Is this going somewhere? Get to the point, I hear my inner voice mutter. But because I am committed to *listening* as a State of Being, I work hard not to interrupt. I breathe, notice my feelings, smile in recognition of my own impatience and my desire to *listen* well. Current studies on the psychological and physiological effects of smiling suggest that in addition to lighting my orbitofrontal cortex, smiling lights up my left anterior temporal region, an area associated with positive affect; and my left parietal region, an area responsible for verbal communication and activity. Neurotransmitters, dopamine, endorphins, and serotonin are released when I smile and feel the smile, or embrace the idea of a smile. My body relaxes, and my heart and blood pressure may lower.

I hear Yeats whispering in my ear to be still and silent. I *listen*. And wait. I am reminded, that like Cage's work, there may be no apparent point. Yet. Sometimes a leader simply needs to tell their stories. As writer Joan Didion says, "We tell ourselves *stories* in order to live." The leader's job is to tell their *story*. My job is to *honor that story* through attentive and intentional *listening*. And begin there.

COACHING MODEL

WHAT: Honor Story

WHY: Listening with the heart and head is at the core of effective coaching. Deep, focused listening, without judgment, is how we gather data, connect the dots, notice tone, create space for leaders to be heard, and sometimes talk their way to understanding and problem solving. Deep listening helps build trust with the leader, an essential aspect of effective coaching. We often hear that leadership is lonely. This is because there is information that leaders can't share with others: hiring, promotion, and firing issues, for example, or personal issues, legal matters, and other sensitive topics. Frequently, the only person the leader can talk to about these is the coach.

HOW: Listen

Begin with Self
- Begin the session with See the Higher Self (Coach to Assets)
- Throughout the session, notice your own feelings and silently name them in order to manage them. Notice your breathing and other cues that indicate you might be feeling distracted, stressed, or triggered, so that you *can quiet your ego* and *be present* to the leader. Intentional breathing, shifting your position in your chair, and placing both feet on the floor can help you reset.

With the Leader
In person: Notice unspoken cues and facial expressions. Listen to word choice, tone, pauses, and breathing. Adapt your own listening cues through easy eye contact and natural, responsive gestures and/or facial expressions.

By phone: Listen to word choice, tone, pauses, breathing, and other vocal sounds that you have learned about how the leader processes. Offer your own occasional responses to help the leader know you are listening.

- Wait through silences to allow for processing time.
- Try not to interrupt unless the leader gets stuck in a pattern.

41

Be Curious
- Ask authentic—not leading—nonjudgmental questions to gather data, build trust, promote a safe environment, and encourage self-reflection.
- Ask "What's clearer to you now?" any time you get stuck, or want to have the leader reset or synthesize for clarity.
- Consider issues that arise, then identify the most pressing or salient strand(s) that need(s) attention, or ask the leader to identify it/them.
- Offer back to the leader what you heard, including perceived meaning and assumptions.

Before Moving On
- Make a note of topics discussed, key details you want to retain for the future, and next steps.
- Ask: "What's clearer to you now?"

Supporting States of Being
- See the Higher Self (Coach to Assets)
- Be Curious (Ask Nonjudgmental Questions)
- Be Present (Remain Unattached to Outcome)
- Appreciate That Everyone Has a Piece of the Truth (Gather Perspectives)
- Acknowledge Mystery (Trust Intuition)
- Quiet the Ego (Check In before Checking Out)

Potential Traps
- Allowing judgment and your own emotions to cloud listening
- Interrupting
- Being distracted
- Rebutting rather than responding
- Making assumptions
- Being attached to outcome
- Solving the problem for the leader
- Forgetting that *everyone has a piece of the truth,* including the person(s) cited in your leader's story

Chapter 4

Be Curious
Ask Nonjudgmental Questions

> *My coach's questioning techniques allow me time to*
> *answer my own questions as well as make decisions*
> *on my own as a leader, without leaning on someone*
> *else to make them for me.*
>
> —School leader

URGENT SCHOOL LEADERS CAN RARELY make time to pause, reflect, and consider questions—big and small. Dedicated coaching sessions provide that space. We have to make good use of leaders' precious time by asking informed, nonjudgmental, non-leading questions that gather data, push thinking, and guide them to do the heavy lifting toward solving problems. Thoughtful questions that are *unattached to an outcome*, can elicit transformational aha moments for the leader. Some of the questions and prompts below can be turned into declarative, *bold* statements depending on whether you are building a relationship with the leader or have an established, trusting one.

Asking Nonjudgmental Questions

Coaching is most effective when done with the purity of seeking to understand, without judgment, allowing curiosity, experience, and intuition to guide us. This requires us to *be unattached to outcomes*, which requires that we don't ask leading questions; instead, state what you're thinking to check for understanding. One way to make sure the questions are received in a nonjudgmental way is to substitute the words *what* or *how* for *why*. Instead of asking, "Why did you do that?" I might ask, "What were the factors that informed your decision?" or "How did you come to understand that?" By asking What or How, we take the sharp teeth out of the Why question, transforming it from feeling potentially accusatory to the leader, to helping her come to her own understanding of her decision-making process, which is the transformation we're coaching to.

A Meditation on *Be Curious*

Understanding that I need to continue to build a trusting relationship with leaders through our conversations, I engage in questions that propel the conversation forward, calling on some of the prompts found in the coaching model at the end of this chapter. Some of these questions/prompts are gleaned from the many coaching sessions I have engaged in, and others were contributed by the coaches I have supervised over the years. All the prompts/questions are informed by States of Being and the 7EQs

It was during my work as the founding host of two public radio programs (*The State of Things* and *Do No Harm*) that I discovered the power of silence when engaging one-on-one. If I sat in silence, even for a few seconds after guests answered a question, they would inevitably expand on the answer they had just given. And often, it was in these moments that the rich, and sometimes unexpected, material would emerge. In my first coaching session with Julian, for example, he revealed after a silence, "I don't like telling teachers what they're doing wrong, and telling them what to do. I just didn't know how else to do it." This offered me the data I needed to know how to coach him.

COACHING MODEL

WHAT: Be Curious

WHY: Coaching is most effective when we seek to understand, not judge. When we coach through genuine curiosity, we discover what the leader knows, believes, feels, and assumes. We discover what they have tried in the past, what has worked, and where they are stuck now. Being curious helps us gather data, push thinking, and guide leaders to do the heavy lifting toward solving the problems or challenges they wrestle with. The prompts below are designed to this end. Some of the prompts can be turned into declarative statements, depending on whether you are building a relationship with the leader, or have an established, trusting one. Note that rather than ask *why?*, questions begin with *how* and *what*. This takes the sharp teeth of judgment from the question. We can still *be bold*.

HOW: Ask Nonjudgmental Questions

Begin with Self
- Before your session: Imagine the person at moments when you saw or heard them succeeding.
- Inhale *listen* / exhale *compassion*.
- Begin the session with See the Higher Self (Coach to Assets)
- Throughout the session, notice your own feelings and silently name them in order to manage them. Notice your breathing and other cues that indicate you might be feeling distracted, stressed, or triggered, so that you can *quiet your ego* and *be present* to the leader. Intentional breathing, shifting the position in your chair, and placing both feet on the floor can help you reset.

With the Leader
In person: Notice unspoken cues and facial expressions. Listen to word choice, tone, pauses, and breathing. Adapt your own listening cues through easy eye contact and natural, responsive gestures and/or facial expressions.

By phone: Listen to word choice, tone, pauses, breathing, and other vocal sounds that you have learned about how the leader processes. Offer your own occasional responses to help the leader know you are listening.

- Wait through silences to allow for processing time.
- Try not to interrupt unless the leader gets stuck in a pattern.

Prompts

Prompts to get grounded and/or propel the conversation forward

- What success, big or small, have you experienced since we last spoke?
- Last time we spoke about _____.What success have you had with _____ since that time?
- What is clearer to you? (This question serves me more frequently than most. The leader's answer helps me when I'm stuck and don't know where to go. It also helps them clarify what they know and synthesizes what they are learning.)
- If you did know, what would you say? (This question can be used in response to the colleague saying "I don't know." It almost always allows them to "know" by giving them a little distance, as if they were coaching someone else.)

Prompts to specifically coach to equity

- How are you beginning with self to examine implicit and explicit biases?
- What does an equitable school look, feel, and sound like for students, staff and families?
- How are you creating a sense of belonging?
- What are you doing to create conditions for students, staff, and families to feel free to be authentic?
- What are you doing to inhibit the creation of conditions for students, staff, and families to feel free to be authentic?
- How have you recently noticed and/or acted upon opportunities to interrupt systemic racism?
- How are you actively creating equitable schools, organizations, and communities?

- What are the power dynamics?
- Who has a voice? Who doesn't?

Prompts that seek specific, transactional information
- What have you already tried? (*Imbue them with their own intelligence*)
- How have you solved other similar problems? (*Imbue them with their own intelligence*)
- What's at stake? (This helps them get to the heart of the matter)
- Are there things you are worried about regarding the process or outcome?
- What is your job as you understand it?
- Do you have the tools you need?
- Do you know how to ask for what you need?
- Are you focused on an outcome or an end in mind?
- Do you know what's expected of you?
- How do you know you're being effective?
- What are the consequences of this decision or action?
- Does your staff know the Why?
- Do your students understand the Why?
- Is it urgent?
- Is right now the right time to act?
- Can you sort the tasks you identified by importance?
- What's your strategy?
- Do your teachers know what is expected of them? (This is a hallmark of teacher satisfaction and development.)
- How do you spend your time with teachers?
- What are one or two things that you choose as priorities for your school?
- What can you delegate?

Transformational prompts that seek to understand, provoke reflection, and help clarify
- What would you like me to know? (This question gives the leader control of the material.)
- Tell me more about that.

- I'm wondering...
- What makes this situation important to you?
- How are you feeling? (Make the distinction between feeling and thinking.)
- If you were coaching someone about this challenge, what would you tell her?
- How would you rewrite that movie scene? (This offers them an opportunity, with distance, to consider a new way of handling a situation that didn't go well.)
- How do you foster relationships?
- What does success look like?
- How will you know when you're successful?
- How do you articulate your vision?
- What do you find challenging about leadership? (This is a big question.)
- What parts of your work give you the most pleasure and satisfaction?
- Which parts don't?
- What are you encouraged by?
- How do you usually solve problems?
- Are you thinking as a teacher or a leader? (New leaders often need help making this distinction.)
- When you coach teachers, what are you learning?
- Are you spending time on the things that advance your vision/mission?
- What are you doing that's having the biggest impact on students?

Observational prompts anchored in being bold
- A *pattern* I notice is...
- Drama is seductive
- That's a strong reaction.

Prompt without language
- Silence. (Silence allows reflection, particularly for people who are introverts. Silence often elicits rich information.)

Prompts for self-care
- Are you taking time for yourself? Is it in your calendar?
- How are you taking care of your physical self? Emotional self? Spiritual self?
- Are you getting enough sleep?

Check for Understanding
- Is this helpful?
- What do you need more of? Less of?
- Test suppositions
- Reflect back to the leader what you heard including perceived meaning and assumptions.

Supporting States of Being
- See the Higher Self (Coach to Assets)
- Honor Story (Listen)
- Be Bold (Hold Their Hand While You Hold Their Feet to the Fire)
- Be Present (Remain Unattached to Outcome)
- Appreciate That Everyone Has a Piece of the Truth (Gather Perspectives)
- Quiet the Ego (Check In before Checking Out)
- Acknowledge Mystery (Trust Intuition)
- Interrupt Patterns (Notice Repetition)
- Imbue Others with Their Own Intelligence (Help Them Connect the Dots)

Potential Traps
- Asking leading rather than curious questions
- Overreliance on asking questions when being bold and interrupting patterns would be more effective
- "Why" questions can sound accusatory and cause defensiveness
- Asking multiple questions at a time is confusing
- Asking sarcastic or judgmental questions, such as "Shouldn't you find a way?," "Why did you do that?," or "What's the point of that?"

Chapter 5

Be Bold
Hold Their Hand While You Hold Their Feet to the Fire

Be gentle and you can be bold.

—Lao Tzu

WE HAVE A MORAL AND ETHICAL obligation to be kind and bold. Urgent schools make big audacious promises to students and families, promising to interrupt intergenerational poverty through education—to help children become their and their family's aspirational selves by going to and through college, and to realize their dreams. There are times when leaders have to *be bold* with a colleague to rise to these promises. When we are kind and *bold* with leaders, it teaches them how to do the same with their colleagues when they have to, for example, *interrupt a pattern*—theirs or a colleague's—or notice that a teacher isn't meeting expectations. Perhaps the leader has to have a conversation with a colleague who insulted someone with a microaggression, or undermined the team. It is imperative that *being bold* is driven by the motivation for the leader to become the highest vision of themselves, and not driven by anger or being *attached to an outcome*. Or held captive by fear when a leader has to fire someone. *Being bold* is a key to that freedom.

It becomes less daunting to *be bold* and make hard decisions when we aren't confused about who our stakeholders are. For me, it's the students and families, with the leader as the primary conduit. When I keep this at the center, my palms are less sweaty and my heart beats more evenly. I reduce fear and can *be fully present*.

Holding Their Hand While Holding Their Feet to the Fire

Sometimes we have to identify issues that leaders may not bring to the coaching session—issues that may not be on their radar yet that we recognize are critical to their leadership development. We can hold both: the leader's highest self *and* areas of growth and development. To illustrate this duality in action, an emerging leader I coached offers this observation in an evaluation about our coaching relationship:

> I appreciated my coaching with my leadership coach, because she supported me by holding up a mirror of not only what she knew I could become, but also a mirror of the personal struggles that would prevent me from getting there. My work with my coach helped me to believe that I could be a better version of myself, not because she told me so, but because she would point out the moments when I was moving in the right direction. But she was also able to uncover my blind spots, helping me to break patterns that were limiting my view of my potential for myself and others with whom I worked.... My coach re-

spected me enough to tell me when I was stumbling. I can remember several coaching sessions where I received feedback about the language that I used to talk about others, and situations of challenge. While it may have stung to hear that my language was indicative of judgment deeper than I cared to pay credit, I knew that my coach was offering some insight into some of the operating principles that were limiting my ability to access my greatest yet to be. It was through these coaching conversations, that my coach told me the hard truths. It was in these sessions that I noticed in real time how I was quick to categorize colleagues as obstacles rather than allies. In these candid conversations, we were able to deconstruct why this had become my method of operation and how it would hinder my ability to reach the goals I had for myself. Through this direct coaching, I came to trust my coach in inexplicable ways, because I knew she respected me enough to tell me when I was messing up. Her honesty was not about giving me the answer, but helping me to find my own answers by uncovering parts of myself I chose not to notice, whether consciously or subconsciously. Moreover, I had access to understanding myself in ways that I wouldn't have otherwise had if she had not been so forthright.

When we consistently hold our leaders' highest selves in front of us—and in front of them—with the end in mind to coach them toward becoming fully authentic leaders, we can *be bold* with confidence. It is the *compassionate* thing to do.

Conversations about equity can be complicated and challenging, especially when the coach is white and identifies as straight, and the leader is a person of color or identifies as LGBTQ, or visa versa, unless there is deep trust.

When I engage in conversations in areas of race, class, gender, and sexual orientation, I bring with me my own intersectionality—my history and my ancestors' history. My awareness and my blind spots. I have to constantly be scanning my biases. And, I have to sometimes name that I am doing so. My approach to *being bold* about equity is twofold: (1) Bring these conversations to leaders rather than wait until they introduce them. Sometimes this can be done by first *asking nonjudgmental questions* to gather data. This process leads to an examination of beliefs and attitudes, and their impact on colleagues, students, and families. Using the 7EQs as entry points is helpful. Sometimes you can begin the conversation simply by making an observation. (2) Build trust to make space for leaders to safely find ways to give voice to their experiences. This is increasingly challenging with shifting language, identities, boundaries, understanding, and experiences. With all the leaders I coach, the objective is anchored in bringing these conversations to the forefront because, after all, equity is the business we are in. I use the 7EQs to guide me, understanding that "we" includes me. I've repeated the 7EQs here, because they are so foundational to *being bold*:

1. How are we beginning with self to examine our implicit and explicit biases?
2. What does an equitable school look, feel, and sound like for students, staff, and families?
3. How are we creating a sense of belonging?
4. How are we noticing and acting on opportunities to interrupt systemic and structured racism?

5. What are we doing to create conditions for students, staff, and families to feel free to be authentic?

6. What are we doing to inhibit conditions for students, staff, and families to feel free to be authentic?

7. How are we actively creating equitable schools, organizations, and communities?

A Meditation on *Be Bold*

In one of my early sessions with Julian he began to reflect on how he was feeling about the way he approached leadership:

> I realize that the development of myself takes just as much work as I put into the development of other people. As a kid and as a high school student or college kid, I was never known as the stern, stoic Julian that was very, like, boom-boom-boom [he rhythmically punctuates this by tapping his closed right hand against his open left palm]. I was so relaxed and easy-going and so able to get along with everybody. It's only in my work life that this [stoic] reputation has emerged. And it's also because of work that I spend drastically less time around people that I used to know who would reinforce the authentic person that I think I am. It makes me wonder how far away from my real self I have gotten because I'm paying so much attention to what I'm doing. When I'm around my family or friends . . . I literally feel totally different. I don't like some aspects of the reputation that I have, and it follows me everywhere I go. But I figure I can hide behind that and get done whatever I need to get done. I'm starting to recover myself in all of my interactions. I'm wondering why I am just coming to this realization now.

Here is this accomplished, young African-American man making himself vulnerable to me, a man who is trying to lead when he feels as if he has to park his authentic self at the door. That he has to hide out. It feels so wounding to hear this. This is a travesty for leaders who need to be fully themselves, to feel whole and be utterly *present* in order to influence and guide colleagues, children, and their families. *Trusting my intuition*, I sensed I would need to *be bold*. Here are excerpts from our recorded 80-minute coaching call which took place in 2013.

> LB: (Using the State of Being *Be Curious*) I have some ideas (about why he's just coming to the realization above), but I have some questions first. Did you grow up in a Black community in school and at home?
>
> JULIAN: Yes.
>
> (I recognize that both of us are about to fearlessly walk into delicate territory, each step a test of our trust, our cultural awareness and competency, of each other, and where the terrain might lead us—a young Black man and an older white woman.)
>
> LB: So, what came to me while you were talking is, "How far away from who I am have I gotten?" is the question you ask, and I wonder if it has anything to do with moving out of the comfort of culture into a white world of work where all Black men have to figure out, How do I move around in here? What are they expecting of me? Can I show who I really am? These are the messages we get growing up . . .
>
> JULIAN: Yeah.
>
> LB: . . . about identity. And I just wonder if any of that rings true.
>
> JULIAN: Definitely. I mean the questions of competence, the questions of safety, all these things I consider when people are

around me so I can't reinforce stereotypes, but at the same time, I can't trade the passion I really feel for certain things, so it's weird. It's really weird. And I never had a model for it. My father is definitely not the model for the kind of things I'm trying to do. My grandfather, he passed about five or six years ago, and he gave me what he could but he was from a different generation. But the core messages were very clear and pervasive. And I've had other examples throughout life but certain things I haven't, like how to . . . how to navigate the professional world. The only example I've had is my mom, and she's talked me through as much as she could, but the rest of it has been through a lot of self-discovery, through some triumphs and some mistakes. I have spent so much time being concerned about how I'm being perceived that it dominates (heavy emphasis on *dominates*) a lot of my interactions with people. And it's exhausting.

LB: It's exhausting.

JULIAN: And I think I'm just. . . , you know. (He describes the scene from *Carlito's Way* in which Al Pacino's character gets out of jail, where he had been seeing a therapist, and says, "You don't get reformed, you just run out of wind.") And I think that's it. I'm tired of doing that. So it's not like I'm changing because of some monumental realization, it's just because it's exhausting. I'm tired of doing it.

(I wanted to give Julian a safe space to unburden himself and also find a way to help him navigate the labyrinth he seemed to feel trapped in. I can empathize but not identify with what he feels. Part of my work as a coach is to help leaders solve their own problems. I decided to focus on his desire to feel and be authentic.)

LB: (Sighs) Yeah. (Silence). So, the question is then, What's in it for you to hold on to this other persona you put forth?

JULIAN: Ah (as in a revelation). What's in it for me to hold on to? (He repeats my question slowly and reflectively.) The space, distance, between myself and a lot of my professional interactions with folks. Although even as I say it, I don't know how healthy that is. Because I'm not totally present.

LB: Mmm (I'm feeling pained with him).

JULIAN: What I wrestle with is, Does that space provide me with safety? Or does it leave a constant roadblock between me and whoever I'm interacting with?

LB: It seems that one question you'll have to ask yourself is, What am I afraid of?

JULIAN: Yeah, and the first thing that comes to mind is being seen as that incompetent, overaggressive, irrational leader. Not meaning to sound arrogant but I think I put in enough time where—these people have kept me around and kept hiring me for something so . . .

(We both laugh.)

JULIAN: They didn't keep me around for my sense of humor, so it must be something else, so (laughter). . .

(We talk through some previous successful experiences he had as a leader when he felt free and authentic.)

LB: This is as plain as it can be, Julian. When you free yourself up to be your authentic self, you give permission to everybody else to do the same.

JULIAN: Mmm (recognition and revelation). Wow! I'm writing that one down.

LB: They're taking their lead from you. The more you free up with David (a principal Julian supervises), the stronger he's going to get. You may already be seeing some of that.

JULIAN: I'm going to work on me, but I like where he's going, I like where all three of them (principals he supervises) are going.

LB: You have a lot to do with that as you work on you. I want to say two things before we end here. One of them is that I have unbelievably deep admiration for you for taking on the development of self.

JULIAN: (quietly) Well, thank you.

LB: Oh, my gosh, that's a big journey.

JULIAN: I feel like it's the only real important one.

LB: Well, it is the only thing you can do. I mean, really, we have control over nothing else. Except who we are. And we don't always have control over that. You have grown up over your formative years internalizing all the messages about Black males. And you had to do the dance of, Where do I feel safe being who I am?, and, by the way, am I sure about who I am because I'm internalizing a lot and I don't know what's real and what isn't? I mean that's just part of what we do when we work through . . . when we work . . . when we feel like we have to match some sort of identity that. . . . We're all multiple identities.

JULIAN: Yeah.

We talk through a challenge he is having with his manager, a white male, how Julian perceives the manager, and how Julian thinks he's being perceived. We name previously identified strengths to leverage in order to have more productive conversations with this manager. I'm aware, with a kind of heaviness, that as is most often the case, the person of color has to do the heavy lifting toward equity. I feel like I want to name that I recognize this, but I don't bring this to the current conversation because we're getting near the end of our session, and I don't want to take us down another road. My intention is to help Julian act on what he has come to understand in this session, and to help him move forward.

LB: What's clearer to you?

JULIAN: Definitely in being very specific about the feedback I ask for, and the idea that I give permission to others to be authentic when I am. That's a huge takeaway for me. And acknowledging that my upbringing adds to my current confusion, but I have the ability to figure it out.

(Over time, Julian would come to understand that his confusion was rooted in the conditioning and messages he received during much of his upbringing and also in inherited pain and hypervigilance from some of his family members.)

LB: So here's what I would say: Try asking for feedback (from his manager) first where the stakes are low.

JULIAN: OK.

LB: (*Imbuing him with his own intelligence*) And only you know what that looks like.

JULIAN: And believe it or not, that's my time with my individual principals. They get all of me, and we both enjoy it.

LB: And I'll bet you're energized after those sessions.

JULIAN: Very much so.

LB: And, I imagine you have more energy for your family on those days.

JULIAN: Yes!

LB: So you'll have to notice the places, Where am I not doing that and what can I do about that?

JULIAN: Yep.

LB: Got it?

JULIAN: Got it.

LB: We'll talk soon.

JULIAN: Thank you, Linda, talk to you soon.

It has not been a straight line toward reclaiming himself since then, but these revelations made it possible for Julian to begin to feel authentic, whole, and heard. He has become more confident in his boldness and desire to be his full authentic self. To put a stake in the ground. He has since moved into equity as his primary work in schools across the country, engaging others in very *bold* conversations, including me.

COACHING MODEL

WHAT: Be Bold

WHY: We expect schools to make bold promises to students and families: to foster their vision of success through high quality and equitable leading, teaching, and learning. Bold promises require bold leadership. And coaching. This means we sometimes hold a mirror to leaders, driven by our desire to see them become their highest self. It is less daunting to *be bold* when we are utterly clear that students are why we do this work. Our palms are less sweaty and our hearts beat more evenly when we keep this at the center. Being bold can build trust when we have consistently demonstrated that we have the leader's best interest at heart.

HOW: Hold Their Hand While You Hold Their Feet to the Fire

Begin with Self
- Before your session: Imagine the person at moments when you saw or heard her succeeding.
- Inhale *listen* / exhale *compassion*.
- Begin the session with See the Higher Self (Coach to Assets)
- We can sometimes anticipate, plan, and practice *bold* conversations, but often they arise in the moment.
- Throughout the session, notice your own feelings and silently name them in order to respond with the end in mind to *coach the leader to her higher self*. Notice your breathing and other cues that indicate you might be feeling distracted, stressed, or triggered, so that you can *quiet your ego* and *be present* to the leader. Intentional breathing, shifting your position in the chair, and placing both feet on the floor can help you reset.

With the Leader
In person: Notice unspoken cues and facial expressions. Listen to word choice, tone, pauses, and breathing. Adapt your own listening cues through easy eye contact and natural, responsive gestures and/or facial expressions.

By phone: Listen to word choice, tone, pauses, breathing, and other vocal sounds that you have learned about how the leader processes. Offer your own occasional responses to help the leader know you are listening.

- Wait through silences to allow for processing time.
- Try not to interrupt unless the leader gets stuck in a pattern.

Be Curious
- Ask, "What's clearer to you now?" any time you get stuck, or want to have the leader, or you, reset or synthesize for clarity.
- After making a *bold* statement, *honor story* and *be curious*. Support the leader in exploring their understanding of the situation. Help her leverage strengths to make needed change.

Be Compassionate
Boldness and kindness can and must coexist. Before responding, make sure it's from a place of kindness, not from anger or judgment, or from your own triggers. It's particularly important to notice yourself during *bold* conversations and take cues from your breathing and muscle tension. As noted above, notice what your facial expression is communicating, even if you are coaching by phone; facial expressions translate to voice. Microaggressions and macroaggressions challenge our capacity for compassion. This doesn't mean you shouldn't acknowledge your feelings; it does mean that you remember that your end in mind is to coach the leader toward her highest self.

Examples of declarative statements to practice compassion (for the leader and for self):
- "I need a moment to process or absorb where we are."
- "I'm feeling triggered and need to take a moment."
- "I can imagine how this [what the leader just said] might have landed on the teacher."

Be unattached to a specific outcome
As you listen to the leader, a solution may present itself to you. Make sure you're coaching to the leader's end in mind and not to the outcome you want.

- "I've heard you complain about this teacher during our last three coaching sessions. What do you want to do about it?"

Trust Intuition
Being bold is a relative experience. What feels bold to one coach may not feel bold to another. Similarly, leaders have different levels of sensitivity to boldness.

Interrupt Patterns
Name the behavior you observe while holding a vision for that colleague's higher self.

Examples of direct, succinct statements:
- "Practice saying that long explanation in two sentences."
- "When you say _____, I hear a fixed mindset."

Examples of direct statements followed by a question to allow the leader to absorb and respond:
- "A strength of yours is asking for feedback. What keeps you from using that approach with your colleague?"
- "You committed to doing _____. You didn't do it. What happened?"
- "I don't hear you owning the development of your leaders. What do you need to do to make that change?"

Engage with the 7EQs
- "When you didn't respond to the teacher's comment, can you see how you missed an opportunity to interrupt racism/ sexism/etc?"
- "The new policy you instituted has the potential to undermine your commitment to creating a sense of belonging."

Before Moving On
Ask: "What's clearer to you now?"

Supporting States of Being
- See the Higher Self (Coach to Assets)
- Be Curious (Ask Nonjudgmental Questions)
- Be Compassionate (Walk in Their Shoes)
- Honor Story (Listen)
- Acknowledge Mystery (Trust Intuition)

- Be Present (Remain Unattached to Outcome)
- Imbue Others with Their Own Intelligence (Help Them Connect the Dots)
- Appreciate That Everyone Has a Piece of the Truth (Gather Perspectives)
- Quiet the Ego (Check In before Checking Out)

Potential Traps

- Being attached to the outcome
- Probing through curiosity rather than naming what you hear and see
- Allowing your ego, anger, or impatience to drive your conversation and responses
- Needing to be right or to even a score
- Using the situation to gain power
- Being conflict averse

Chapter 6

Be Present
Remain Unattached to Outcome

*And yet as a coach, the most we can hope for is to
create the best possible conditions for success then let
go of the outcome.*

—Phil Jackson

WE COACH TO THE TRANSFORMATIVE end in mind, not to outcomes, because outcomes can change. A way to make the distinction between "end in mind" and "outcome" is this: End in mind is aspirational or transformational, for example, fostering the love of learning. Outcomes are specific or transactional, for example, resulting test scores. Another way of distinguishing between outcome and end in mind is that outcomes are determined by circumstances, situations, and sometimes by the successful completion of a previous outcome. So, a transformative end in mind might be to create conditions for students, staff, and families to thrive. One outcome of that end in mind might be lower attrition rates. From there other outcomes might emerge: higher rates of successful college attendance, or increased family engagement, or strong literacy achievement. As legendary NBA basketball coach Phil Jackson suggests in the quotation above, coaching requires us to *be present* to the process of transformation, *to let go of outcomes.* In his autobiography, he says, "I often reminded the players to focus on the journey rather than the endgame, because if you give the future all your attention, the present will pass you by." This reminder to *be present* is critical to learning how *to let go of outcomes,* particularly when leaders feel so much pressure from external sources to "produce results." It's hard to argue with an historic 13 championships (11 as a coach, two as a player).

Remaining Unattached to Outcomes

Perhaps of all the States of Being, this one, in my experience, has been the most challenging for leaders and coaches to grasp. Leaders frequently have difficulty envisioning how they will drive results if they aren't attached to them. Recall Julian's story at the beginning of this book, where he continued to tell his math teacher what to do in order to get his students' scores up. By focusing so intently on the outcome, he lost sight of how to "create the best possible conditions for success," as Jackson puts it. Like most leaders, Julian lost his authentic self in the linear drive toward achievement. And he didn't like how he felt.

I hear stories like Julian's every day.

Coaches are challenged to *remain unattached to outcome,* as well, because we can feel certain that we have the right answer. Or we might believe, like Julian or Sonya did, that progress only comes from telling rather than from asking or guiding. We might become impatient or view people as obstacles rather than allies while what we should be doing, most of the time, is coaching others to find their own way—their own answers—*imbuing them with their own intelli-*

gence. But how do we do this? Even the most seasoned among us has to continue to learn and practice what's at the core of this challenge. *Remaining unattached to outcomes* while helping others find their own way does not mean we don't offer advice anchored in our experience. It does mean, however, that we tap our experience in order to respond to the leader's needs, not to impose our own solutions to a problem. This is an ongoing dance.

Julian struggled with the idea of *remaining unattached to outcomes* from the outset of our coaching sessions: "How can I let go of outcomes and still hold people I manage accountable, and get results?" He discovered his own answer through our work together, through his work with the principals he supervises, and by coaching two school leaders I assigned to him. When I review our notes over time, I think his own trajectory best demonstrates how to embrace this State of Being. Early in our coaching relationship, I asked him to tell me about a success, big or small, that has helped him learn to *be present* and *unattached to the outcome*.

> JULIAN: I definitely would say my conversations with my two coaching leaders (the two I assigned to him). They have opened up tremendously. Both are in very different places. I feel like I'm starting to get better at meeting the individuals where they are and not going into manager/advice-giver/mentor mode but trying to stay in questioning mode—trying to push myself to ask better questions and trying to keep my mouth shut as much as possible and let them guide themselves to the answers. Agreeing to be a coach is giving me a better perspective on understanding my own leadership style and on how to inspire and motivate others to be their best selves. I keep going back to that. That's what helps me keep my mouth shut. The coaching session isn't for me per se; it's for them to improve as leaders. So, I focus on how do I help them come to the conclusions for themselves.

(Here is the framework of his strengths that I gleaned from his story. I read these back to him: Meet them where they are. *Be Curious. Imbue Them with Their Own Intelligence.* Focus on helping them to be their highest selves. I write these strengths in the imperative tense so he can use them to address future challenges.)

LB: Is there anything else that comes to you? (People almost always have more insights after they hear their strengths read back to them.)

JULIAN: Uh . . . um . . . paying attention to my own *listening.* And trying—it's almost like separating the thoughts in my mind as I'm listening to what am I processing and what am I forming as far as a follow-up question to what they're saying. What am I summarizing for them? You know, it's like three or four different thought tracks or avenues going at the same time. Trying to keep track of them all. A lot of it is through repetition and getting used to it. I think the experience as a principal lends itself to it. I have to keep track of different priorities at the same time but this one is even more intense because I have a very quick touch with them (leaders) every two weeks, and I want to make it as meaningful as possible without sort of giving them the key—giving them the answer that I think is the correct answer.

LB: (I add *Honor Story [Listen]* to his list of strengths.) And so what I'm wondering is how does this translate to your work on the ground (with the principals he supervises, as opposed to coaches)?

(Julian and I are collaboratively coaching toward his development as a leader—the transformational end in mind. His work as a coach is part of the process.)

JULIAN: So, working with principals—it really is helping me develop and incorporate my coaching perspective and lens with my managerial lens. Even before that, I think the biggest thing I have so far learned is that there is so much to appreciate about the differences in the leadership styles of the people I work with.

Julian goes on to say that as he *coaches to his principals' strengths*, he is building and deepening his relationship with them, *listening* well, and making it possible to *be bold* when he has to engage in tough conversations with them. He holds them accountable to the steps they agree on and discovers that they are more productive as a result of his new approach. He is building trust, an essential aspect of leading effectively. I add *See the Higher Self, Be Compassionate*, and *Be Bold* to his list.

A Meditation on *Be Present*

Julian found himself at a crossroads again a year later when the stakes were much higher. One of the principals he was supervising and coaching in his district was struggling, and the board was concerned. Julian had reached an impasse. He had run out of ideas. This time, with the principal's permission, he invited me to sit in on one of their one-on-one meetings. His goal was "to have you help facilitate a conversation that would allow me to get to the root of the difficulties that I'm having in motivating and supporting this particular principal." A few minutes into the session, I could see that Julian had gotten himself stranded in the outcomes that shut down his *intuition, listening*, and *compassion*, while the principal seemed to be suffering.

I first noticed Julian's and the principal's (we'll call him "Charles") demeanors. Julian's rhythm was percussive and crisp, his voice and jaw strong, and I recalled how I felt when I first sat across from him a couple of years earlier. Charles's rhythm was slow and tentative, his voice quiet, and spine slightly slumped. He answered all the questions with no affect. Julian was working the drums while Charles was blowing a mournful sax.

After their initial exchanges about the most recent steps Charles had taken to try to get his team to rally around a commitment to excellence with their students, I noticed he began to shift his gaze toward the floor. Julian hesitated, sat back in his chair, sat forward again, made a few comments, and asked Charles if he had any questions. "No, I'm good." Julian was clearly doing most of the talking and heavy lifting in the conversation.

I was recalling Julian's earlier struggles with being his authentic self and felt him drifting toward the man who was expected to be stoic and to get things done—"Boom-boom-boom." Internalized voices are hard to ignore. Here he was, sitting with another African-American man with whom there was mutual affection and respect. Something else was going on here. I felt the need to *interrupt the pattern* they were in. At the point when Charles said, "No, I'm good," I asked if I could enter into the conversation. They both seemed relieved.

"You've both been working so hard," I said. "So hard. And yet, there is no significant change. You both must feel very frustrated." Like a rehearsed duet, they quickly and emphatically responded, "Yes!" I asked, "Would you like to explore this?" Again, "Yes." My *intuition* told me that Charles was feeling sad and shamed. With *compassionate boldness*, I noted this out loud, and Charles began to weep. The authentic Julian knew what to do. "I'm sorry, man. I'm sorry I missed this because I was driving toward outcomes and forgot to figure out how to help you do what you do best." They spoke with each other about their feelings, their worries, the reason they both do this urgent, difficult work. They were two men, sitting together as equal partners, making space for each other's hearts and minds. I sat in silence, as witness.

One year later, Julian shared this reflection about the session:

> About a year ago I was in a very difficult position. While supporting a principal I was working with, I had to *hold his feet to the fire* as far as outcomes for the school. I had tried many technical/tactical approaches such as helping him work on his weekly schedule, his meeting agendas, and observing him as he was meeting with his team members. However, I still wasn't seeing the progress necessary that was going to have a positive impact on student outcomes. I felt there was some sort of block or gap between how I was supporting him (through modeling, practice, and sharing best practices) and his understanding of how to implement my suggestions and models.

> Through the course of this conversation [real-time coaching session], it became clear that not only was this principal deeply internalizing the mounting pressure that was being exerted on him from myself, my supervisors, and the board, he was unable to clearly identify his difficulty implementing change, and that was leading to crippling self-doubt and anxiety. The clincher was that he felt as though he was disappointing me, and that was paralyzing to him (as he looked up to me not only as a boss, but as a role model). Once this realization was reached during this session, I apologized for not allowing him total access to my impressions of his potential, and my firm belief in his ability to do this job. He needed to know that my

pressure on him came from a place of genuine belief in his ability to get it right and was authentic. I had to tell him that I had not written him off. It almost felt like a parent reassuring their child after a major disappointment that "everything was still going to be ok." I had to do that while still being very clear on what needed to be done (outcomes).

What became clearer to Julian:
No matter what I tried to do for this principal, I needed to first acknowledge where he was emotionally (anxiety and crippling self-doubt), speak openly about my role in creating this state, and allow him space to process those feelings.

In other words, Julian acknowledged their interdependency. During the coaching session I attended with the two of them, I put several States of Being to the test, gliding and weaving, guided by the end in mind to coach these two men to *see their own and each other's highest selves.* Two years later as Julian moved into more senior leadership, he shared the following:

For a very long time it was hard for me to separate my coaching responsibilities (building capacity in the people that I was supervising) from my management responsibilities (ensuring I hold them accountable to the directives essential to the successful completion of their jobs). Through my coaching experiences, I started to understand that there really isn't a separation between the two. The art of coaching is trying to figure out how to leverage both personal and professional strengths that my coaches possess, so they can then apply them to their job responsibilities. I became better at understanding how to do this effectively by being coached myself. This helped me to continuously look at my strengths, and with confidence, build the framework of how to apply those strengths regardless of the pending task, project, or conversation. Sustainability in my job comes primarily from effectively managing the stress connected with my job responsibilities (supporting principals). Through my experiences being coached, and coaching others, I've more consistently abandoned a deficits-mindset in myself and my direct reports. Those who I supervise (who are mostly coaches themselves) have begun to adopt many of my new habits related to building strength-based frameworks. This is proof-positive for me that I'm building capacity, and thus becoming a more effective leader and leadership developer.

Julian came to understand that transformation drives transaction and outcomes, not the other way around. In other words, the transformation Julian was hoping for with Charles—to get him be a more productive, successful leader—was thwarted by getting stranded in tactics like schedules and agendas.

People change. Even as they are telling their story, what they first thought and felt can change by the time they get to the end of it. Julian began our first coaching session by telling the story of how he coached using the "shit-sandwich" model. By the end of the session, he realized that he wished he had *coached to the teacher's assets* and that, perhaps, he might not have had to fire him. In his work with Charles, he realized that he had to access his authentic self in order to allow Charles to access his. Outcomes can change.

But what do we do as coaches when we know that the leader is going down the wrong path? For example, I know that the "shit sandwich" is not a productive coaching technique. By engaging *Quiet the Ego (Check In before Checking Out)*, I noticed that I felt a sense of judgment about it. I then recalled the time I fired my whole staff when I was a young leader, a memory that enabled me to access compassion to replace judgment. This is one of the most challenging aspects of coaching—to understand rather than judge. To *check my ego*, and my own values and beliefs, and use them as a guide or compass but not impose them. I'm not always successful.

This isn't to say that I don't have opinions about what effective supervison and leading look like. I do. But if I say to Julian, "It's not a good idea to use the 'shit-sandwich' model; it's a better idea to do it this way [fill in the blank]," he will have no reason to accept this, or more importantly, to implement it. He must come to his own realization through *nonjudgmental curiosity*, while being *coached to his highest self, imbuing him with his own intelligence*, and *remaining unattached to outcomes*. Then, I can offer him the tools to implement the strategy.

One might think, "This is all well and good, but we have to drive results—that's our end in mind." But, as we discussed at the beginning of this chapter, end in mind should not be confused with results. Recall that end in mind is aspirational or transformational (love of learning); results are specific or transactional (test scores). Often, these two approaches are incompatible at best and undermining at worst. I have been in many urgent schools that devote whole days to preparing students to take standardized tests; they have test pep rallies and other high-energy activities, which may be energizing for extroverts but enervating for introverts. Some schools even have competitions for the best scores among grade levels. When we focus on the process of learning and discovery, outcomes—test scores— generally take care of themselves. Remember what champions do: Their aspirational end in mind is to walk into their most important games able to perform both physically and mentally at the highest possible level, but their focus is on one pass, one block, one possession at a time, not the score, not the standings. Their end-in-mind process is to learn how to play to their strengths, build trust and unity as a team, run drills over and over to keep skill-levels high, draw up and practice plays and debrief them with the coach to figure out how to improve. That's how Phil Jackson coached his teams to 11 championship rings.

A coach's job is to guide people to their own discovery so that the experience is transformational, not transactional. Otherwise, we will be right back at the table, problem-solving how to get the next teacher to implement a lesson plan, or a leader to get results. Julian is passionate about getting his teachers to succeed so their students will, as well. He has a kind heart, is self-aware, and wants to learn as much as he can. This is the man I see. This is the man I coach to.

COACHING MODEL

WHAT: Be Present

WHY: We coach toward transformational change, or an end in mind. Paradoxically, we have to stay focused on the present moment to get to the end in mind, or we risk skipping over essential information along the way. When a coach becomes attached to an outcome without realizing it, she is unable to stay present to the story that the leader is sharing and may miss or even inadvertently redirect the leader's true end in mind.

HOW: Remain Unattached to Outcome

Begin with Self

- Before your session: Imagine the person at moments when you saw or heard her succeeding.
- Inhale *listen* / exhale *be present.*
- Begin the session with See the Higher Self (Coach to Assets)
- Throughout the session, notice your own feelings and silently name them in order to manage them. Notice your breathing and other cues that indicate you might be feeling impatient or certain that you are right, so that you can *quiet your ego* and *be present* to the leader. Remind yourself to *listen* and to *be curious.* Intentional breathing, shifting in your chair, and placing both feet on the floor can help you reset.

With the Leader

In person: Notice unspoken cues and facial expressions. Listen to word choice, tone, pauses, and breathing. Adapt your own listening cues through easy eye contact and natural, responsive gestures and/or facial expressions.

By phone: Listen to word choice, tone, pauses, breathing, and other vocal sounds that you have learned about how the leader processes. Offer your own occasional responses to help the leader know you are listening.

- Wait through silences to allow for processing time.
- Try not to interrupt unless the leader gets stuck in a pattern.

Quiet the Ego
- *Check in with your feelings and thoughts before checking out* with a response to a specific outcome that you think is the only one that will work.
- Silently notice and name your feelings. Smile in recognition of the feeling.
- Remind yourself to *be curious*.
- See her as an ally.
- Breathe. Shift in your chair.

Honor Story
Stories change as they unfold; therefore, outcomes can change. We have to listen for and notice subtle shifts in tone, language, silences, posture, and occasionally tears. Listening well requires us to be fully *present* and *compassionate*, otherwise we will miss these cues.

Imbue Others and Be Curious
Leaders know their schools, teachers, students, staff, families, and communities better than we do. If we are *attached to outcomes*, we run the risk of viewing the leader as an obstacle to solving the problems we think need to be addressed, rather than engaging with her in an interdependent coaching relationship of discovery.

- Commit to guiding her to her own solution rather than driving towards your prescribed outcome.
- *Ask nonjudgmental questions* to collect data and build trust.
- Allow the leader to think and talk her way to resolution and aha moments.

Examples of being attached to an outcome and unchecked ego:
- "I know this will work. I've coached other leaders to do this, and it worked for them."

Examples of shifting to imbue her with her own intelligence:
- "Here are some of your strengths we have identified over time. Which ones can you call on for this situation?"
- "If you did know, what would you do?"
- "What's clearer to you now?"
- "What have you heard from parents about this situation?"

- "Do you have exit interview data that shed light on this problem?"

Supporting States of Being
- See the Higher Self (Coach to Assets)
- Honor Story (Listen)
- Be Curious (Ask Nonjudgmental Questions)
- Appreciate That Everyone Has a Piece of the Truth (Gather Perspectives)
- Imbue Others with Their Own Intelligence (Help Them Connect the Dots)
- Quiet the Ego (Check In before Checking Out)
- Be Compassionate (Walk in Their Shoes)

Potential Traps
- Certainty that your answer is the only right one
- Believing that progress only comes from telling rather than asking
- Being impatient
- Focusing only on results
- Viewing people as obstacles not allies

Chapter 7
Be Compassionate
Walk in Their Shoes

Sympathy is not that productive in terms of helping
people learn. For me sympathy is saying something
like, "I am really, really sorry for what has happened
to you." The unspoken part of that is, and I am
really glad that it is not happening to me. I have
been to a funeral and you say to a person, "Oh, I am
so sorry." But the unsaid is, and I am really glad it is
not me. What I am trying to get teachers to cultivate
is empathy, informed empathy, that says I know
what it feels like to be in this very same situation.

— Dr. Gloria Ladson-Billings

WHEN THE WORK IS URGENT, moving at a fast pace, and the stakes
are high, it's so easy for leaders to slip into impatience and judgment
about an assistant principal who gets angry, or a teacher who doesn't
seem to be measuring up. About one who isn't fitting in. Who doesn't
seem to "get it." It can be hard for coaches as well when a leader we

coach doesn't seem to be making progress. In these moments, it's hard to access empathy and so easy to forget what it was like to be new at our job, to be a first-year teacher or leader, or to just be having a bad day. Or to not have the tools we need.

In these moments, it's important to remember that most teachers and leaders come to work every day with the desire to help students learn, grow, and become the best versions of themselves. To make good choices. Or at least they started out with that intention. If we want leaders—and those they lead—to succeed, it's essential to *walk in their shoes* so that we can understand where they are and then guide them toward their highest self.

The next time you hear yourself sigh at someone, or shake your head with impatience, or write someone off, remember what your first year on the job was like, or the time you lost the attention of your classroom, or said something ridiculous in a meeting.

Walking in Their Shoes

Practicing compassion is a challenging pursuit: It demands of us that we suspend judgment by understanding what triggers it in us and how to manage it. It requires us to *be present* to others' suffering while maintaining our capacity to engage with it in a constructive way, if we are to be of help. And, most importantly, it requires us to connect to the feelings of the other person rather than distance ourselves from them. For that, we must know the difference between sympathy and empathy, a distinction so clearly articulated by Ladson-Billings in the quotation above.

We *practice compassion* by recalling times that we have struggled, failed, questioned our own competence, and also by recalling times when we needed a friend or a lifeline and were met by one who dwells in the realm of, Is it kind, true, and thoughtful? Does it speak to the highest self? We *practice compassion* in coaching to better understand the leader's perspective, help them feel understood, and build trust.

Without making it about us and by keeping the focus on them, our ability to feel *with* them communicates, "Your story is my story; your pain is pain I understand."

A Meditation on *Be Compassionate*

I am swirling inside the centrifugal force of transformation, my own and as witness to others. I brought Bidyut ("BK") Bose, researcher, scholar, and founder of the Niroga Institute, to work with 18 leaders to help them reflect on themselves and their response to the urgent and demanding work they do. Bose's work is anchored in neuroscience and yoga-based practices. He helps people find intentional ways to respond to stressful situations rather than simply react to them. His protocols are healing: to stop, to breathe, to notice the self, to move. Healing helps make this work sustainable.

In their session with Bose the leaders receive an overview of the brain's physiological response to stress; they come together to name a vast array of stressors (both large and small, common and uncommon); they identify things that sustain and nourish them; they learn and practice breathing and other yoga-inspired exercises. I can feel the mind and spirit of the room begin to change, the quality and depth of which happens too rarely in the intense and rapid-response life of the leader. Bose helps them understand that while they can't always change events that occur, they can choose and manage the way they respond. The leaders reflect on times they have jumped to unproductive interactions with students and staff because they were unaware of their own stress and therefore unable to set aside their judgments or *practice compassion*. They discover how they might have managed the situation if they had understood this. They begin to see how their stress creates barriers to their own humanity and to their compassion for others.

We often wonder how many of the tools and ideas we offer our emerging leaders they actually use when they reenter their schools and immediately get swept back into the unrelenting demands of the work. After this session, it was very clear. In my individual coaching calls with the leaders the following week, I discover that they are still steeped in aspects of the training, not only practicing it themselves but already introducing it to their teachers and students.

Here is one of the articulated visions I received from a leader. A white elementary-school assistant principal in an urban school, "Celia's" previous schools had failed her Black students academically, emotionally, and spiritually. Celia left the workshop with this end in mind: "I identified and made myself aware of my biggest dream: to make our school a place where we heal before we teach and truly engage children in critical thinking, and have excitement about learning." The elegant universe offered her the opportunity to practice immediately on Monday morning.

During our next coaching session, she reports that she heard a colleague yell at a third-grader for falling asleep in class. I *check in before checking out* to manage my judgment about this vivid scene. *Imbuing her with own intelligence*, I ask what she thinks would cause a teacher to yell at third-graders. She thoughtfully reflects and says, "They are frustrated with themselves for not being prepared enough. And because students don't change their behavior."

She then reports that, with her new tools and insights from the workshop, she approached the student and chose to *listen* to him: Heal before teaching. "What's going on, Quinton?" He tells her that he can't sleep at night and has gruesome, graphic dreams. He says that since his father left and his mother went to jail, he's afraid his aunt and grandmother, with whom he lives, will also go away. He's on high vigilance all night and falls asleep during class. This 8-year-old, unburdening himself, was able to shift into engagement with Celia, a seasoned leader who is deeply dedicated to straightening the crooked room of education. She asks him what he's interested in. "Science," he offers. Celia calls his aunt and receives permission to bring Quinton home late because she wants to take him to buy a science book.

The next day, Celia asks him how his night was. He excitedly reports that he loves his new book and after reading it, fell into a deep sleep. Quinton let go of his nightmare, and Celia, in this moment, is living her dream.

She and I then talk about a third-grade class that is so difficult that a very seasoned teacher walked out. She describes a chorus of "whining." Refrains of "Why should I have to give the pencil back to Jondre? He stole mine first!" kind of whining. Calling on *compassion* and my own experience to respond to Celia's dilemma, I suggest to her that third- and fourth-graders are at an age where they become very aware of justice, and this is one way they express it. I offer her resources of stories and films about justice and about transforming anger into productive interactions that teachers can use with students. They can then role-play because practice is a bedrock tool of trans- formation. She responds with a kind of awe: "I had never thought of it that way. Justice! Never thought that this might be what they were expressing." Celia is lit up. On fire. Ready to see her students in a new light. She also understands that healing is a process, and that Quinton has a long way to go. And so do the teachers she coaches. She under- stands that her transformational experience with Quinton was a mo- ment in time. Our next session will focus on (1) *coaching her teachers to their highest selves*; (2) teaching them to *listen* to students' stories by *listening* to theirs; (3) modeling for her teachers the practice of *asking nonjudgmental questions* so they can do the same with students. She recognizes that the teachers have to heal before teaching as well.

We end our call with intentional breathing together. And I'm still swirling in the transformation, living my own dream out loud— seeing the potential cascading impact of coaching.

COACHING MODEL

WHAT: Be Compassionate

WHY: It's important to remember that teachers and leaders come to work every day with the intention to help students learn, grow, and become the best versions of themselves. If we want leaders to succeed, it's essential to walk in their shoes so that we can understand where they are, what keeps them up at night, and what tools they need to succeed. Only then can we begin to guide them toward their highest self.

HOW: Walk in Their Shoes

Begin with Self
- Before your session: Imagine the person at moments when you saw or heard him succeeding.
- Inhale *listen* / exhale *compassion*.
- Begin the session with See the Higher Self (Coach to Assets)
- Throughout the session, notice your own feelings and silently name them in order to manage them. Notice your breathing and other cues that indicate you might be feeling judgmental, so that you can *quiet your ego* and *be present* to the leader. Intentional breathing and shifting in your position in the chair can help you reset. Smiling, or the feeling of a smile, can also help you reset.

With the Leader
In person: Notice unspoken cues and facial expressions. Listen to word choice, tone, pauses, and breathing. Adapt your own listening cues through easy eye contact and natural, responsive gestures and/or facial expressions.

By phone: Listen to word choice, tone, pauses, breathing, and other vocal sounds that you have learned about how the leader processes. Offer your own occasional responses to help the leader know you are listening.

- Wait through silences to allow for processing time.
- Try not to interrupt unless the leader gets stuck in a pattern.

Honor Story
- *Listen* with *curiosity* and for discovery, without judgment.
- Remember what your first year on the job was like, or a time when you struggled, failed, felt sad, questioned your own competence, felt lonely, lost the attention of your classroom, or said something ridiculous in a meeting.
- Breathe, step into the leader's shoes, and *coach to their strengths*.
- Provide space for the leader to think and talk her way to understanding.

Be Curious
Ask nonjudgmental questions to collect data and build trust.

Examples of what compassionate curiosity sounds like in a statement:
- "That must have felt _____."
- "Tell me what would be most helpful to you right now."
- "It sounds like you were being courageous."

Examples of what compassionate curiosity sounds like in a question:
- "What strengths have you called on in other situations like this?"
- "Who are your lifelines?"
- "What self-care do you practice?"
- "So that I know how to listen, do you need to vent for a while, or do you want to try to solve the problem?"

Supporting States of Being
- See the Higher Self (Coach to Assets)
- Honor Story (Listen)
- Be Curious (Ask Nonjudgmental Questions)
- Acknowledge Mystery (Trust Intuition)
- Be Present (Remain Unattached to Outcome)

Potential Traps
- Being impatient
- Getting triggered
- Being impulsive
- Confusing your issues with theirs
- Mining their deeper psychological issues

Chapter 8
Interrupt Patterns
Notice Repetition

When you review or practice something you've
learned, dendrites actually grow between nerve cells
in the network that holds that memory.
—Judy Willis

ONE OF THE INTERESTING THINGS about patterns is that we often
don't recognize we have them until confronted by a particular stimu-
lus. For example, a leader might not be aware that she has a pattern
of avoidance. After all, she went charging ahead when she decided to
open a new school or when she became a successor leader of a school
that was failing its students. She steps into the middle of a student
fight or volunteers to deliver a Ted Talk on the power of interrupting
intergenerational poverty through education. But ask that same leader
to have an authentic conversation with a teacher who is late every day
or an assistant principal who triangulates staff members against another teacher? Or with a teacher who believes that her students aren't

learning because they're African-American or Latina/o/x? Suddenly, that fearless leader who forged through three feet of flooded, snake-invaded classrooms after a recent hurricane, gets weak-kneed. We discover, through coaching, that she has practiced avoiding engaging in authentic or consequential conversations with teachers. She has done this by practicing reflex techniques that are now stored in her memory network where, as suggested by neurologist Judy Willis in the quotation above, dendrites have taken root. Neuroscience shows that repeated negative thoughts and mental processing eventually create corresponding physical networks in the brain. Or, as Willis says, "practice becomes permanent." As daunting as that sounds, however, she reminds us that we have the same power to create new connections between nerve cells by choosing to reinforce healthy, positive, success-promoting patterns.

When coaching, it's important to pay attention to repetition or recurring patterns of behavior or language that can interfere with or undermine a leader's influence. Or stall their growth, progress, or the implementation of their vision. Or perpetuate unrecognized internalized biases they have been socialized into, as in the example above regarding beliefs about African-American or Latina/o/x students. Patterns are learned, and we want to coach leaders to recognize an undermining pattern so that they can unlearn it and make space for a new, productive pattern where new dendrites can grow. Even fearless leaders can be fragile when they first recognize an unproductive pattern, so when we choose *Be Bold* to help a leader *Interrupt a Pattern*, we have to bolster that boldness with *compassion*.

Noticing Repetition

At times, patterns are obvious: A leader might regularly blame others when things aren't going well for him, or he might default to making jokes when meetings get tense. Patterned behavior can be subtle. For example, he may not respond to emails or might not acknowledge or greet his staff members when walking down the hall, causing them to feel unseen, dismissed, and unappreciated. Or perhaps he might get sullen or disengage.

Sometimes, leaders deepen their patterns by repeating the story they tell themselves over and over, like, "I'm conflict-averse." This pattern has the capacity to inhibit growth by giving legitimacy to the character and the circumstances they have created. They can get stuck in their own story, and the pain it may have caused them, through the act of repeating it. My response is to acknowledge the pattern with the end in mind to help the leader interrupt it: how we get there will be *by imbuing them with their own intelligence*. But first I have to *listen* so that I can assess whether the person seems ready to begin the healing process and decide if we're ready to take it on at that moment.

It also depends whether we are working one-on-one or in a group; on when in the conversation the pattern presents itself. If it's toward the end of a coaching session, this can be a challenge to address. Picking it up at another time is also a challenge, but possible. I have had a few sessions with different leaders during which I had to take what felt like a giant risk to *trust my intuition* and *be really bold* to *interrupt the pattern*, even when second-guessing myself.

When I become aware of a patterned behavior in a leader, I first *check in before I check out* with them and silently acknowledge any feelings or triggers I may have—judgment, for example. Perhaps I feel annoyed that the leader bounces from topic to topic whenever we begin to talk about their pattern of avoiding authentic or difficult conversations with a teacher. Reminding myself that all coaching roads lead back to leadership, and *focusing on the leader's highest self*, I then ask myself, "What is the transformational end in mind to coach to?" To help the leader recognize the pattern that is interfering with their leadership, and coach them to unlearn it and replace it. I *cannot be attached to an outcome*—a particular new behavior that they should have. Rather, I will *imbue them with their own intelligence* to figure out the How.

When coaching, we want to help the leader make discoveries about how these patterns could be interfering with their ability to solve problems, have more productive relationships with colleagues, and fulfill their aspirational vision of themselves.

A Meditation on *Interrupt Patterns*

The person with patterned behavior is more practiced at it than we are at responding to it. Or interrupting it. Patterned behavior works because of the dependability of the response. It's rare that the leader will be asked by people they supervise to stop joking and address the tension; instead, they might laugh along with the leader—the dependable response. It's almost certain that no one will call a leader out for yelling; they will usually shrink and comply. It's difficult to speak truth to power. Our job as coaches is to *interrupt the pattern* by naming it.

As a coach, it's important to view patterned behavior as a response that the leader has been practicing for a long time because it may have served him in the past. It may have even saved his life. Perhaps he joked as a way to get family attention, for example. Or perhaps he learned to keep his head down or hide to avoid an angry, abusive parent. In his role as a leader, however, this behavior no longer serves him, and we want to guide him to see how a pattern of making jokes, or remaining silent, or yelling isn't accommodating leadership. This doesn't mean that we should mine his childhood looking for clues to his pattern. We aren't therapists. Instead, we notice and acknowledge the behavior through literal notes that we've taken during coaching sessions and through observations. We have to help the leader be aware of the behavior in order to release and replace it.-

It's also important to remind myself to feel gratitude and *compassion* for his wisdom of developing a pattern that may have once served him. The fearless leader who avoids having authentic conversations has learned to make jokes at inappropriate times as a learned, reflexive response. My intention, or end in mind, is to help the leader recognize and interrupt the pattern by *asking nonjudgmental questions, being bold and kind, trusting my intuition,* treading carefully, and *remaining unattached to the outcomes,* such as how long it might take or what he chooses to replace it with.

The first step is to name the pattern by giving an example of it. Then I identify the kind of impact it may have. In this scenario, I offer: "I notice that you have a great sense of humor and that can be a useful asset to diffuse tension. Most assets have shadows as well. I notice a pattern that you tend to make jokes when we begin to talk about an authentic conversation you would like to have with a teacher but have been avoiding." I offer him examples—literal notes—from our coaching sessions. After a moment, I *ask a nonjudgmental question*: "Do you recognize this pattern?" Then I say, "It's possible that this pattern likely served you well in other areas of your life for reasons that you may or may not recognize."

The leader almost always recognizes and acknowledges the origin of the pattern, but I offer: "It's only important that *you* understand where the pattern developed; I don't need to know." I make it a point to offer this option to leaders—that they don't have to tell me deeply personal things, and I don't invite them to for two reasons: (1) I'm not a therapist and don't want to imply that I can address these issues; and (2) our work together is to stay focused on leadership—on the present, not the past.

I might ask, "I'm wondering if you can see how making jokes might be the way you avoid having authentic conversations?" The leader almost always begins to acknowledge this kind of observation.

I ask for an example to make sure he understands and/or is not giving me a response he thinks I want to hear. On the rare occasion they are unable to, I refer to previous coaching notes as data and offer specific examples. We're moving into sensitive territory because he understands that I see him in ways that likely haven't been acknowledged before. He has built strong defenses because his attention hasn't previously been brought to this. It's so personal. I offer my gratitude for his willingness to bring up an uncomfortable situation he has just exposed. Then, because I want to make sure I am not driving into territory without his permission, I ask: "Would you like to address this pattern?" In all the years I have been coaching, no leader has ever said no. Leaders want to evolve to their highest selves, and they express gratitude, sometimes relief, for the opportunity. If there is trust.

I'll offer something like this to the leader: "Our job together is to find a way to unlearn and replace this behavior to serve you and your staff more effectively: a way for you to be in charge of the pattern so it's not in charge of you. Would you like to do that?" I always ask a leader's permission to engage in reshaping a pattern. It's *compassionate* and considerate, and I want him to feel in charge of it as a way to model how to take charge of a behavior that currently has power over him.

I explain that replacing one behavior with another one is key when trying to change it. When we give up smoking or luscious desserts, for example, we are most successful when we replace the cigarette or chocolate brownies with carrots or fruit. It may be unsatisfying for a while but eventually we feel better, can breathe more comfortably, smell better, and look and feel healthier. The cigarette gave us a jump-start, the brownie was comfort food, but they both made us feel bad in the long run. We've broken a pattern that has served us for some time.

I then ask the leader what he would like to replace the behavior with. Leaders almost always know what they would like to do because *everyone has a piece of the truth. Imbued with his own intelligence,* this leader says he would like to replace his jokes with silence. I recommend that he try that until our next coaching session in two weeks, then check in to see how it went. I suggest that he practice in low risk situations. He seems eager to try this. I also invite him to email me if he would like to, to let me know how it's going, or for support.

When we next speak, I will narrow the frame of my opening *coaching-to-assets* question: Tell me a success, big or small, when you interrupted your pattern of making jokes.

COACHING MODEL

WHAT: Interrupt Patterns

WHY: Patterns are learned. Often, they have served people in the past, but now may be interfering with leadership. Sometimes patterns are developed unconsciously without any connection to having served the leader before. We interrupt the leader's patterns to open new, more effective and productive ways of leading. When a leader becomes aware of her own patterns and works to shift them, she tends to be more empathetic with colleagues whose patterns interfere with their work and has the tools to interrupt them.

HOW: Notice Repetition

Begin with Self

- Before your session: Imagine the person at moments when you saw or heard her succeeding.
- Inhale *listen* / exhale *compassion*.
- Begin the session with See the Higher Self (Coach to Assets)
- Throughout the session, notice your own feelings and silently name them in order to manage them. Notice your breathing and other cues that indicate you might be feeling distracted, impatient, stressed, or triggered, so that you can *be present* to the leader. Intentional breathing and shifting in your chair can help you reset. So can smiling.

With the Leader

In person: Notice unspoken cues and facial expressions. Listen to word choice, tone, pauses, and breathing. Adapt your own listening cues through easy eye contact and natural, responsive gestures and/or facial expressions.

By phone: Listen to word choice, tone, pauses, breathing, and other vocal sounds that you have learned about how the leader processes. Offer your own occasional responses to help the leader know you are listening.

- Wait through silences to allow for processing time.
- Try not to interrupt unless the leader gets stuck in a pattern.

Honor Story

Listen and watch for recurring patterns of behavior that may be interfering with progress. These might be things like routinely forgetting to thank people for their work, making jokes during serious moments, reacting instead of responding, being indecisive, doing everything herself, forming combative relationships, among many other patterned behaviors.

Be Bold and Compassionate

- Name the *pattern* and the impact for the leader so she can begin to recognize it.
- Check to see if she recognizes the pattern: it's only important for her to understand the origin of this pattern, it's not necessary for us to know in order for her to interrupt it.
- Acknowledge the beauty of the pattern that might have once served but now interferes with effectiveness.
- Ask if she wants to change the pattern.

Examples of declarative statements about noticing patterns:
- "I notice that you make a joke when you begin to practice having an authentic conversation with a colleague."
- "This is the third combative relationship you've had with a colleague."

Be Curious

Examples of nonjudgmental questions about patterns:
- "Are you aware that the way you describe the interaction with your colleague was reactive rather than responsive?"
- "Is this pattern familiar to you?"
- "Would you like to try to change the pattern?"
- If the leader would like to change the pattern, ask, "What would you like to substitute the behavior with?" (Replacing a behavior offers the most successful way to interrupt it.)

Supporting States of Being

- See the Higher Self (Coach to Assets)
- Be Curious (Ask Nonjudgmental Questions)
- Be Bold (Hold Their Hand While You Hold Their Feet to the Fire)
- Be Compassionate (Walk in Their Shoes)
- Acknowledge Mystery (Trust Intuition)
- Appreciate That Everyone Has a Piece of the Truth (Gather Perspectives)
- Imbue Others with Their Own Intelligence (Help Them Connect the Dots)

Potential Traps

- Wanting to fix the leader
- Being attached to outcome
- Being judgmental
- Asking for personal information about the history of the pattern

Chapter 9
Acknowledge Mystery
Trust Intuition

> *For it is intuition that improves the world, not just following the trodden path of thought. Intuition makes us look at unrelated facts and then think about them until they can all be brought under one law. To look for related facts means holding on to what one has instead of searching for new facts. Intuition is the father of new knowledge, while empiricism is nothing but an accumulation of knowledge. Intuition, not intellect, is the "open sesame" of yourself.*
>
> —Albert Einstein

THERE ARE MANY THEORIES ABOUT intuition. It's a form of data—information we gain through experience, tucked away and called on when needed. It's the ability to read environmental cues by hearing the intention behind the words that leaders use, words beneath the words. It's picking up on microexpressions, the nearly imperceptible, fraction-of-a-second, involuntary shifts in facial expressions that reveal real emotions. Intuition bypasses the act of conscious thinking. It's the voice that whispers to us seemingly from nowhere. Intuition is available to all of us in coaching, especially when we accumulate expertise through practice. But as Einstein says above, "Intuition is the father of new knowledge, while empiricism is nothing but an accumulation of knowledge." If we transfer Einstein's theory of intuition to coaching, we could say that we call on intuition in order to transform the accumulation of our experience from a simple index of "unrelated facts" into insightful and productive "new knowledge."

Many explanations of intuition place it in subordination to or supplemental to logical reasoning, revealing the primacy of logic as a bias in Western thought. Taoism, on the other hand, is an ancient and mystically oriented trend of thought rooted in intuition. Taoists believe there are limits to rational thinking; in fact, Taoism has as much of a mistrust of conventional knowledge as conventional science has historically had for intuition. In both Eastern and Western schools of thought, intuition tends to be linked to emotional honesty, and, as we've seen time and again in this book, emotional honesty is critical to effective coaching. Regardless of which theory we subscribe to, what's important is to discover how best to access intuition for use in coaching.

Trusting Intuition

To access my intuition, I have to be awake, open to possibility, to "unrelated facts." In advance of coaching sessions, I actively prepare, or make space, for the intuition by asking for guidance through meditation. A cluttered, tired mind can inhibit intuition, so I do my best to get good sleep. Being rushed or stressed inhibits intuition. The breathing at the beginning of calls I do with leaders—four-count inhale/eight-count exhale and setting an intention with them—also helps clear the mind to be fully present. I also eat well and monitor caffeine intake. All these actions contribute to my focus and to what's at the threshold.

It takes a fair amount of trust to allow images to emerge and to pay attention to them. I have learned to notice words that sometimes suddenly float into my consciousness, or song lyrics, or a poem that might intrude, or an image I suddenly see forming. During a coaching session, I sometimes close my eyes and just feel and notice. Also, I will sometimes ask a leader for a silent moment so I can take notice of what's going on in my body or what's being offered to me. The more I embrace *remaining unattached to the outcome*, and work to *quiet my ego*, the more intuition presents itself.

I don't entirely understand how images come to me, or why I get a particular feeling about someone, but I don't question how I get unseen or unspoken information because judgment clouds intuition. It is the enemy of intuition because it's irrationally rational, and intuition requires an open pathway. I have come to *acknowledge mystery* and accept that information does come to me. It is available to all of us.

Sometimes the words or phrases or a line of poetry or song lyrics that present themselves to me have no immediate meaning until I offer them to the leader as a form of data. It is almost always the case that they immediately understand the significance, or interplay with their current situation. I manage the information carefully, staying as neutral as possible to help further the coaching process, not to test my own skills. That would feel unethical and ego driven. *Quiet the Ego (Check In before Checking Out)* is a State of Being that I acutely practice. I have come to trust the information I get through intuition because it is so often validated by the people I coach. What I have come to understand is that my intuition is not working independently of my thinking. They are working in tandem as my intuition scans the accumulation of seemingly unrelated facts and generates new knowledge.

It takes practice and intention to cultivate intuition. We do this by getting quiet so we can hear our inner voice. There are practices that help: Make sure we're rested. Begin and end the day naming things we're grateful for—as small as the light on a leaf, and as expansive as feeling loved. Actively observe our environment. Keep a journal—even a few sentences, particularly when we notice coincidences or when things feel as if they are in perfect alignment. Meditate. Notice what's happening in our bodies, especially when coaching. Pay attention to dreams.

It's also important to note that inducing positive feelings enhances intuition, whereas negative moods diminish it. This is how *See the Higher Self (Coach to Assets)* and *Acknowledge Mystery (Trust Intuition)* are intertwined. In order for a coach to *see another's highest self*, we must first enter into a positive frame of mind, which makes it more possible to access *intuition* when coaching. We must then *be bold* enough to act on it.

A Meditation on *Acknowledge Mystery*

I'm sitting with a cohort of 10 rising leaders I've been coaching individually for a few weeks. This is the third day they have come together for the Tell Your Story session, designed to connect their own personal stories to the story of why they choose the arduous work of urgent school leadership. I make sure to set a sacred space with them, defined as giving our full attention to the storyteller (including no electronic devices or writing implements), listening without judgment, not interrupting while someone is telling their story, and keeping the circle intact. We also begin by agreeing, one by one, to confidentiality.

I notice that one of the participants, a white male in his mid-

twenties, is sitting slightly removed from the group. I make a mental note of his posture and presence. He has a tight jaw, a locked,
stiff spine, lowered gaze, shallow breathing, and sparse contribution
to the otherwise actively engaged group. It feels as if he is carrying
around a practiced anger. I scan my *intuition:* Do I address this or
let it go? Then I notice Annie Lennox's "Smithereens" begin to play
in my head. I have come to depend on songs that suddenly come,
unbidden, and I have learned to pay attention. Here are some of the
lyrics to the song I heard in my head:

> Behind the victim
> Behind the trouble
> Are all the things
> You've not expressed
> I see you standing behind your mother
> I see you hiding behind her dress
>
> . . .
>
> 'Cause everybody has a tender heart
> Remember this
> I didn't mean to break it down to smithereens
>
> I heard you crying
> I learned the story
> I saw the shadows behind the past
> They fall behind you
> And creep up slowly
> We're only human
> Behind the mask
>
> . . .
>
> And you say
> Everybody is an island of their own.

He chooses to be the last to offer his story. He tells a bit of one, a story that relies on broad brush strokes, but has no specifics. This helps confirm my *intuition* that he is hiding a key part of himself ("behind the mask") because he had been witness to nine other stories over three days, and had seen the process of offering specific, detailed information. *Checking in before checking out*, I'm not sure if pressing him a little will push him too far. My *intuition* about his untapped anger is not yet informing me. I'm not sure which voice to pay attention to: mine or Lennox's. I don't want to see him "break down to smithereens." I engage his help.

I *check in again before checking out* and *imbue him with his own intelligence*: "I'm not sure if I should press you for more specifics to your story. I don't know what will emerge." I breathe, relax, and notice that I feel more confident now about engaging with him because I was emotionally honest with myself and with him. My *intuition* is now guiding me because I let go of judgment and fear. I notice he has shifted and turned his attention toward me. The room feels thick. Then, I quietly say: "I sense a deep anger. Does that have any meaning to you?" We all wait in silence while he absorbs the shift. I am grateful that I *trusted my intuition* because it invited me to tap into my courage. My observation and clear question allowed him to unfold a story of shame that he needed to tell and purge. We listened with full attention. When he finished, we thanked him for his trust.

He said that he felt grateful to finally release this story and noted that the safety of his trusted colleagues made this possible—it created a sense of belonging to free him to feel authentic. I ask him if he has told this story before. "No," he responds, "not this fully." I offer to the group that in order to lead effectively, it is important for us to embrace the fullness of our stories as part of who we are, to be fully present to lead others. As Eréndira Flores, a leader I coached, so eloquently states: "We have to own our stories so they don't own us."

He and I went for a walk afterward. He expressed relief again. I suggested that he look into therapy to help him find a safe place to investigate his story, to understand his shame and anger, and the impact on his leadership. He said he would think about it. A couple of years later, he wrote to me to let me know that this session had a profound and lasting effect on him and that he had taken steps to heal.

A note of caution: It takes experience and skill to manage these sessions. If I had been less experienced, I would not have asked him about his anger. What if he had exploded? Or left the room? Or engaged in any other possible challenging or potentially dangerous responses to my question about his anger. What I anchored in was years of experience and training with seasoned mentors who know how to navigate these kinds of moments: from how we set them up through how to *remain present* to each person in the room simultaneously, and always with fidelity to the end in mind. In coaching, it is important to know and respect our limits and boundaries.

Part of the process of the Telling Your Story session is that after the teller is finished, we open the circle for people to respond to specific questions: What landed with you? Or, What part of this story felt like your story? Advice-giving is not permitted. The teller simply listens while someone writes the responders' comments so he can be fully present. Then, depending on what transpires during the response time, I might ask the teller if there is anything he needs to ask or say. Then, I bring that storyteller's session to a close with a poem I create by scribing a few words/phrases I heard him offer. Lastly, I ask if he would like to have the poem. No one has ever declined.

Let's discuss for a moment how a less experienced coach could manage the scenario I described above. I would not recommend observing "a deep anger" for the reasons I mentioned above. Instead, a newer coach might ask, "Would you like to hear the group's responses to your story?" If he said yes, the coach could open the circle to the two questions above: What landed with you? Or, What part of this story felt like your story? Then, depending on how that went, the coach might wait a few beats and ask him if there's anything else he would like us to know. During the next one-on-one coaching session, the coach could ask if there was anything about the story session he would like to revisit.

There have been many times over the years of coaching that self-blame and stories of shame have presented themselves. But coaching is not therapy and I am not a therapist. However, through the process of story and self-discovery, buried issues can emerge when people find themselves trusting someone, perhaps for the first time. I will sometimes suggest that a leader work with a therapist—to begin with self in order to *be present* to others—to own their stories so their stories don't own them. *Remaining unattached to outcome*s, and respecting privacy, I will not ask if he decided to seek therapy, or what he and his therapist talk about.

While it may be tempting to want to know details about their past, our curiosity must always be focused on helping our leaders move forward in their leadership. We have to clearly understand the distinction. We do this by *quieting our egos—checking in before checking out*. Finding the intersection between the importance of telling the story, my intuition, and the entry point to interact with it is a constant, delicate, and humbling dance.

COACHING MODEL

WHAT: Acknowledge Mystery

WHY: Intuition is where experience and the unconscious mind converge to inform each other. Intuition can be most effective when coaching unstructured problems—those that don't depend on rules, objective criteria or data. It can inform decision making and problem solving, and is effective when coaching areas that involve human dynamics, like resolving conflicts and interrupting patterns. Intuition helps us sort large amounts of data as leaders talk their way to understanding.

HOW: Trust Intuition

Begin with Self
- Before your session: Imagine the person at moments when you saw or heard them succeeding.
- Inhale *listen* / exhale *be present.*
- Begin the session with See the Higher Self (Coach to Assets)
- Throughout the session, notice your own feelings and silently name them in order to manage them. Notice your breathing and other cues that indicate you might be feeling judgment, distracted, stressed, or triggered, so that you can be *open to intuition.* Intentional breathing, shifting in your chair, and putting both feet on the floor can help you reset.

With the Leader
In person: Notice unspoken cues and facial expressions. Listen to word choice, tone, pauses, and breathing. Adapt your own listening cues through easy eye contact and natural, responsive gestures and/or facial expressions.

By phone: Listen to word choice, tone, pauses, breathing, and other vocal sounds that you have learned about how the leader processes. Offer your own occasional responses to help the leader know you are listening.

- Wait through silences to allow for processing time.
- Try not to interrupt unless the leader gets stuck in a pattern.

Be Present
- *Listen* to and *trust* your inner voice to access what you unconsciously know.
- Read environmental and nonverbal cues to receive what's unspoken.
- When you hear yourself say, "Something tells me..." or "I have a hunch...," this is an intuitive moment.
- Observe judgment rise and watch it float by.

Example of what to say when you have an intuitive moment:
- "As I listen to your story, this phrase (or sentence, or thought) presented itself to me. I'm wondering if it has any meaning for you." (If the leader says no, let it go and move on. It may make sense later.)

Supporting States of Being
- See the Higher Self (Coach to Assets)
- Be Curious (Ask Nonjudgmental Questions)
- Be Present (Remain Unattached to Outcome)
- Honor Story (Listen)
- Imbue Others with Their Own Intelligence (Help Them Connect the Dots)
- Quiet the Ego (Check In before Checking Out)
- Appreciate That Everyone Has a Piece of the Truth (Gather Perspectives)

Potential Traps
- Allowing reason to interfere with the unconscious mind
- Allowing judgment to cloud intuition
- Being attached to outcome, which detaches you from intuition
- Being self-critical
- Feeling stressed, hungry, or fatigued, which blocks intuition
- Allowing an intuitive moment to interfere with listening

Chapter 10
Quiet the Ego
Check In before Checking Out

We must go beyond the constant clamor of ego,
beyond the tools of logic and reason, to the still, calm
place within us: the realm of the soul.

—Deepak Chopra

SEEING THE HIGHER SELF IN others, listening without judgment, and *remaining unattached to outcomes,* requires us to coach from a still, calm place within us, beyond the constant clamor of ego. We do this in order to make sure we are responding to the leader's story and not our own. *Quieting our ego* is also an antidote to believing we have the answers, a trap that *attaches us to outcomes* rather than to the process of discovery.

This means, as Chopra notes above, that we have to broaden our view of the world beyond our own logic and reason in order to *imbue others with their own intelligence* and *honor their stories.* Going beyond the constant clamor of our own ego is how we open ourselves to understanding others—to feel what they feel. In other words, to *be compassionate* so we can *walk in their shoes*.

In order to understand other perspectives, we have to acknowledge and manage our own egocentric ones. Paradoxically, we have to begin with self in order to relinquish our focus on the self. This involves a complex web of thinking informed by experience, feelings, and the lens through which we view the world. For example, if I grew up surrounded only by people who look and think like me, this would inform my perspective. It may influence where I recruit staff, and who I hire. If I were raised in the rural south, I would likely have a different view of the world than if I were raised in Los Angeles or New York City. If I went to private, primarily white schools, I might lead an urgent school differently than I would an affluent school, for example, because of unexamined biases I might have accrued through privilege and exclusion. And so on. Understanding other perspectives takes a lot of internal, ongoing work.

Unexamined ego is intertwined with unexamined biases. If we are committed to creating a sense of belonging and creating conditions for students, staff, and families to feel free to be authentic, it is essential that we have clear access to *compassion*—to the realm of our soul. Leading with ego will block that access.

Checking In before Checking Out

During a coaching session, it is important to continuously check in with our feelings before we offer a response. Am I feeling triggered by something she said? Do I feel judgment rising up? Do I feel angry, frustrated, and so on? When these do come up, silently notice and name the feeling, then smile in recognition of the familiar feeling to release the neuropeptides that will fight stress and help promote health and happiness. Neuropsychologists argue that there is a mutually beneficial effect of the smile: A sincere smile has the ability to both light up the reward center of the brain of the person smiling *and* activate the orbitofrontal cortex in those who see it. So, breathe and choose to *listen* well from a neutral, calm place. It is also important to *check in* with ourselves to make sure we have a handle on our ego: Does my response come from a place that makes me feel smart? Does the session become about me? We want to *check in* with ourselves to make sure we are focused on the leader's development, not on our ego.

A Meditation on *Quiet the Ego*

Some schools in underserved communities have adopted the practice of requiring students, including high school students, to walk in silent, single-file lines as they transition from classroom to classroom. I have also seen schools where kindergarten students are required to walk with "angel wings" (hands behind their backs, elbows akimbo) and a "bubble in their mouth" (puffed cheeks). The stated purpose is to have five- and six-year-old children keep their hands to themselves and be silent. (I could write a whole chapter on how this is developmentally inappropriate with regard to balance and breathing alone, and another chapter on the dreadful recurring example of the need for compliance and control of Black and Brown bodies.)

I am constantly *checking in before checking out*, and sometimes *as* I'm checking out when I engage in these conversations because I have very strong feelings about single-file, silent lines that, to me, seem more like preparation for prisons than classrooms. And more recently, I'm struck by how similar these images are to the lines of children being forced to move in silent lockstep between cages at our southern border. Or witnessing teachers at a high school asking all students moving through a single-file, silent line to lift their outer shirts to show that they are wearing a belt, which is part of the uniform. Another highly inappropriate and unacceptable practice. I have feelings about this.

There was a time when I harshly criticized a few leaders over these issues, and it was hard for us to recover and move forward. I continue to remind myself that although I can't control situations that are presented to me, I can control my response to them. OK. Not always. There are days when I'm tired, or hungry, or weary from the day's news, or I get triggered during the last session of a long, intense day of coaching. When this happens, I tap my emotional honesty and tell the leader what happened to me in that moment. I continue to work at a very conscious level to *quiet my ego* and feed my physiological and spiritual needs.

I began to look at hallway transitions as a way of discovering information about policies, decision-making, and equity. When I engage leaders in these conversations, my end in mind is to explore this. I am led by the 7EQs: How are we beginning with self to examine implicit and explicit biases? What does an equitable school look, feel, and sound like for students, staff, and families? How are we creating a sense of belonging? What are we doing to create conditions for students, staff, and families to feel free to be authentic? What are we doing to inhibit this? Are we noticing and acting upon opportunities to interrupt systemic racism? How are we actively creating equitable schools, organizations, and communities?

Using *Be Curious (Ask Nonjudgmental Questions)*, I'll say, "Tell me about your silent, single-file hallway transitions. What is the end in mind for this practice? The Why?" The responses generally fall within these categories: There may be other classes still in session and we don't want to disturb them. Children have to learn self-discipline, not to bother others. It helps make sure children are safe by keeping their hands to themselves. Or, we have to move quickly between classes; there is no time to waste and they have too much to learn.

I ask how recently they talked with students about the Why. Most often, the leader and I both discover that there has been no recent discussion. This is usually followed by the leader lamenting how much the teachers don't like "policing" them. They often say that teachers have to raise their voices to redirect students, or spend time practicing silently lining up at the doorway. I ask, "What do you think the students are learning with the practice of silent, single-file walking?" Their answer, after a brief silence followed by a sigh, is almost always, "Compliance." To be sure, there is a place for compliance in all organizations, particularly when it comes to safety. Like fire drills and gun violence. When I ask, "Is compliance what you want your students to be learning?," their answers include "no" and "sometimes."

I can hear author/scholar Gloria Ladson-Billings's provocative words echoing in my ear:

> I am a little concerned that they [teachers] would equate regimentation and control for learning. Because that is not what I see when I go to middle class schools.... It bothered me that on the one hand we supposedly know all of this stuff about childhood and adolescent development and yet we won't permit it. I will raise the question of where is the fear of things getting out of control coming from. Other questions might be: How would you feel about your own child making hallway transitions like this? Does the white privileged school across town transition this way? Did you walk this way when you were in school?

Leaders often admit that they don't know what else to do. I'm reminded of Julian's revelation about getting his teacher to successfully implement a lesson plan: "I just didn't know how else to do it."

With regard to hallway transitions, I bring my knowledge of child development to the conversation: children, like adults, are social beings who need to talk and laugh. We can teach them how to do this quietly, and to self-regulate, so they don't interrupt other classes that may still be in session. This is where I offer resources to the leader who "doesn't know what else to do."

As a way to scaffold behavior in the hallways from silent to social, I offer mindful walking and breathing as instruments for learning to self-regulate in a productive way: Notice each step—heel to ball of the foot—students and teachers take, adding intentional, rhythmic breathing as developmentally appropriate. I offer mindful walking because it makes us aware and helps us pay attention with intention. It also allows us to be in the moment without judgment, which helps us focus. Breathing and focusing attention gives students something positive to do while walking side-by-side rather than being restricted: It helps quiet the mind, reset the brain to focus (a fundamental aspect for learning), and reduces stress. Then, students can transition to walking socially but staying mindful with regard to respecting the community's need for quiet around classrooms.

And since the work of education is to teach, and the mind is the seat of learning, we want our leaders to think beyond "this is how it's always been done." Practicing mindfulness has a dual purpose for teachers and students: They both benefit.

I also offer this suggestion because mindfulness is historically practiced in this country by white, privileged communities. Practicing it in urgent schools is a way of making a connection to Ladson-Billings' notion of doing things that many of these teachers would do in their own worlds. It's a response to the essential equity questions. In this case, it's making connections between culturally relevant pedagogy, neuroscience, and hallway transitions.

Then, there's this: Not all cultures are quiet. Some are noisy. Some people need more physical space between each other, some not. Some are more physical with each other. Some do very little touching. Some cultures are more accustomed to arguing, while others are threatened by it. And so on. It is critical to understand the differences before imposing culturally biased policies on students, staff, and families.

There are myriad examples of policies that can challenge a coach's perspective. *Quieting our ego* allows leaders that we coach "to go beyond the clamor" of their own egos, *see each other's highest selves*, honor each other's cultures and practices, *remain unattached to the outcome*, and collaboratively explore transformative possibilities. Here is an example of one leader's responses to our hallway transitions conversation, anchored in the 7EQs and some piece of nearly all the States of Being: See the Higher Self (Coach to Assets), Honor Story (Listen), Be Curious (Ask Nonjudgmental Questions), Be Present (Remain Unattached to Outcomes), Quiet the Ego (Check In before Checking Out), Appreciate That Everyone Has a Piece of the Truth (Gather Perspectives), and Imbue Others with Their Own Intelligence (Help Them Connect the Dots). My end in mind was to coach her to understanding the Why of the school's policy decisions, not to attach to what the policies should be. Because I had *checked in before checking out*, it allowed her to do the same and examine the status quo response, "that's how it's always been done."

I ask, "What's clearer to you, now?"

"I have to begin with self to make sure I have examined my biases," she replies. "I have to think about how to create a sense of belonging in our school, in the classroom, the hallways, cafeteria, and anywhere students are. I have to always consider the Why of the What when making policies and rules. And consequences."

COACHING MODEL

WHAT: Quiet the Ego

WHY: Coaches stand on the balcony to see the wide and active dance floor below. While this offers an essential perspective, it also holds the possibility that we can become attached to an outcome because we have seen the challenge before that the leader presents. Or, we might have had success managing a similar situation a particular way. In essence: we "know" the answer. It is essential that *we check in* before responding to ensure that we are coaching to the leader's needs rather than our own, or the way we would do things.

HOW: Check In before Checking Out

Begin with Self

- Before your session: Imagine the person at moments when you saw or heard her succeeding.
- Inhale *listen* / exhale *be curious*.
- Begin the session with See the Higher Self (Coach to Assets)
- Throughout the session, notice your own feelings and silently name them in order to manage them. Notice your breathing and other cues that indicate you might be feeling distracted, stressed, or triggered, so that you can *quiet your ego* and *be present* to the leader. Intentional breathing, shifting your position in your chair, and placing both feet on the floor can help you reset.

With the Leader

In person: Notice unspoken cues and facial expressions. Listen to word choice, tone, pauses, and breathing. Adapt your own listening cues through easy eye contact and natural, responsive gestures and/or facial expressions.

By phone: Listen to word choice, tone, pauses, breathing, and other vocal sounds that you have learned about how the leader processes. Offer your own occasional responses to help the leader know you are listening.

- Wait through silences to allow for processing time.
- Try not to interrupt unless the leader gets stuck in a pattern.

Listen and Remain Unattached to Outcome
Ensure you are focused on the individual's development, not your need to be right.

Be Curious
Shift judgmental thoughts to nonjudgmental questions.

Example of shifting judgment to being curious internally:
- Judgmental internal commentary: She is not seeing the bigger picture. She's stubborn. I don't know why she can't see the answer.
- Shift to being curious: Silently notice and name your feelings. Smile in recognition of the feeling. Remind yourself to *be curious*. See her as an ally. Breathe. Shift in your chair.

Examples of shifting judgment to statements:
- "I admit to being attached to an outcome. I'm wondering if you could help me understand the end in mind you have for the challenge we are wrestling with." (To remind us that she is an ally, not an obstacle, use we, not you.)
- "I'm wondering if you've gathered others' perspectives that will help us."
- "I need a minute to reset."

Supporting States of Being
- Honor Story (Listen)
- Be Curious (Ask Nonjudgmental Questions)
- Be Present (Remain Unattached to Outcome)
- Imbue Others with Their Own Intelligence (Help Them Connect the Dots)
- Appreciate That Everyone Has a Piece of the Truth (Gather Perspectives)

Potential Traps
- Allowing your ego to drive your responses
- Needing to be right
- Being impatient
- Forgetting she is an ally, not an obstacle

Chapter 11

Appreciate That Everyone Has a Piece of the Truth
Gather Perspectives

The eyes see there materials for building,
See the difficulties, too, and the obstacles.
The mind seeks a way to overcome these obstacles.
The hand seeks tools to cut the wood,
To till the soil, and harness the power of the waters.
Then the hand seeks other hands to help,
A community of hands to help-
Thus the dream becomes not one man's dream alone,
But a community dream.
Not my dream alone, but our dream.
Not my world alone,
But your world and my world,
Belonging to all the hands who build.

—Langston Hughes

WHEN ALL HANDS HELP BUILD the community's dream, the dream belongs to all who help build it, as Langston Hughes so poignantly writes above. This State of Being, dedicated to the belief that *everyone has a piece of the truth*, helps create a sense of belonging when leaders ask their colleagues to serve as thought partners and participate in decision-making. *Gathering perspectives* from teachers, administrators, students, families, and members of service teams is an essential part of creating conditions for employees to feel committed to and invested in the school. This helps them be more productive, go the extra distance, report greater job satisfaction, and stay longer. It helps build a collective dream.

Another benefit is that when leaders strategically invite colleagues to share their perspectives, they are also building the leadership pipeline. This is because they're pulling the curtain back on the kinds of decisions and ideas school leaders wrestle with, preparing their colleagues for leadership roles.

Gathering Perspectives

When we are coaching, it's wise to ask if the leader has received input from others. This query has several benefits: It helps us know what she has already learned so that we can integrate this information into the problem or ideas we're discussing. Additionally, *gathering perspectives* can offer us a window into the school's culture through others' eyes.

It's helpful for coaches to think through with leaders how to be strategic about *gathering teachers' perspectives* so as not to overwhelm them with too much information or responsibility that takes energy or time from the classroom.

Sometimes, when we're coaching, we can feel stymied. During those times, it may even be beneficial for the coach to *gather perspectives* from, say, another trusted coach or colleague. We must be mindful, however, not to breach our coach-leader confidentiality. Always ask the leader for permission to seek counsel.

Some of the most valuable, and often overlooked, perspectives come from students and the dynamic opportunities that present themselves when leaders *see their students' highest selves*, as tillers of the soil, as builders of the community. When we embrace Hughes's vision, the community belongs to "all the hands who build" it. As with adults, *gathering students' perspectives* creates a sense of belonging and grows future leaders.

A Meditation on *Appreciate That Everyone Has a Piece of the Truth*

Part 1

A young assistant principal we'll call Ravelle was quietly influencing change to reflect what she fervently believes schools are for: to create a safe, equitable, peaceful environment where students are *imbued with their own intelligence*, and where they are offered skills and tools to become their highest selves. A place where *students have a valued piece of the truth* regarding their own education. Ravelle believed that this aspiration began with shifting the experience for students who struggled with self-regulation issues. While she had worked with teachers on classroom management/engagement techniques, she felt they were still removing too many students and sending them to her for what were labeled "behavior issues." She recognized she needed more tools. She also wondered if the teachers were acting through implicit biases.

She decided to *gather teachers' perspectives* through the 7EQs. How are we beginning with self to examine implicit and explicit biases? What does an equitable school look, feel, and sound like for students, staff, and families? How are we creating a sense of belonging? What are we doing to create conditions for students, staff, and families to feel free to be authentic? What are we doing to inhibit this? And so on. As staff began to wrestle with these challenging questions, she knew she also needed to offer teachers tools that would help keep students in the classroom.

Ravelle recalled a new perspective she had gathered from a breathing-and-movement PD led by Niroga Institute founder and mindfulness coach Bidyut Bose. She introduced his 15-minute yoga-based protocol to her small reading group, including Dionne, an African-American middle school student who typically got sent to her office because he acted out in class. Teachers had thrown their hands up over him. Ravelle decided to embrace him through the yoga-based breathing protocol, and he quickly began to learn how to self-regulate, a vital key for learning.

During one of these sessions in her office, the principal walked in and the students invited him to join them. He reported feeling calmer afterward and asked Ravelle if she would teach the protocol to the staff. Reminding Ravelle that the community belongs to "all the hands who build," I asked her what it would be like to have Dionne teach the protocol. Ravelle became animated. This seemed like a perfect opportunity to infuse the school culture with a new perspective, build leadership in Dionne, and have his other teachers *see his highest self*, rather than the boy they can't control. Thus, the dream becomes not one man's dream alone, but a community dream.

Part 2

A few days later an email arrives from Ravelle:

> This morning, I ran the idea by our school principal of starting our staff PD with the 15-minute protocol. As we had discussed, I suggested that our student Dionne lead the protocol. The principal was im-

mediately receptive, so I called Dionne's mom. She was beyond excited about the idea: "Oh my gosh, he was just talking about you when he went to his dad's house yesterday. He was showing his dad these breathing techniques, and his dad asked if it was helping him. He told his dad the techniques help him relax and feel focused in school." Dionne will be sharing his experiences with our staff this Friday. This really made my day, and I'm looking forward to the impact it can have on all of us ☺. Have a wonderful day!

Ravelle's small reading group was suddenly influencing the school leader and families who were *gathering new perspectives.*

Part 3
Email from Ravelle the day of the scheduled PD:

This morning, although it started out a little stressful (Dionne's mom had an emergency doctor's appointment but still really wanted him to pursue this opportunity, so we had to make another arrangement for him to get here), went better than I even envisioned. Dionne was calm in front of a group of about 23 teachers, and his presence was awesome. Dionne led us through the protocol, talked about its impact on him and potential impact for others, and then answered questions from this group of teachers. The outcome was other teachers asking if Dionne could also come teach this to groups of fifth-graders, teachers asking me if I could begin working with other students in other grade levels, and Dionne telling teachers that this can be used as a "focus-break in class."

Dionne's sphere of influence and *piece of the truth* was expanding across the school and helping to shift the culture through *gathering new perspectives*. And, his teachers shifted their view of him: from undisciplined troublemaker to leader.

Part 4

I invited Ravelle to present this experience at a PD for another group of emerging leaders. Her school superintendent was present and enthusiastic about the process; he encouraged her to create the next step to deepen the protocol across the school. She and I collaborated on how to continue to build what she had so successfully and thoughtfully begun by helping Dionne demonstrate that *everyone has a piece of the truth*.

Part 5

Ravelle reports that Dionne continues to be focused and calm in school and regularly uses the breathing protocol to help him when he feels distracted or tempted to act out. Since the initial staff meeting, he has presented it to 60 fifth-graders and 80 eighth-graders.

Some time later, Ravelle was appointed successor principal in another school in her district where she integrated the protocol into the curriculum. Her work with students is rooted in creating a sense of belonging, which she achieves in part by *appreciating that everyone has a piece of the truth*—teachers, students, and families alike. She is determined to see all students as leaders by creating conditions for them to feel free to be authentic. She is also engaging her staff in the 7EQs as part of the process.

Ravelle's experience is a powerful example of what it means to expand our understanding of *gathering perspectives*. Before the PD, she knew that there needed to be a change in the way teachers responded to students whom they saw as discipline problems, but she hadn't formulated a plan. A solution began to take root with the vision she created while *gathering perspectives* from Bose and other colleagues in attendance at his PD: "We will build a school where all of us are positively interdependent and respond to each with love and resolve conflict through peaceful resolution." She brought her vision to our coaching session, where we worked on articulating her strengths and ways she could use them to help manifest her vision.

In our coaching session following the Bose PD, knowing that one of her goals was to further develop impact and influence, I narrowed the *coaching to assets* frame: "Tell me a success, big or small, when you shifted a culture."

She talked about having a school-wide impact on academic progress in reading by starting with a philosophy supported by research in order to *gather new perspectives*. She *remained focused on process rather than outcome*. She started small—with one teacher. She described the Why and taught the teacher new skills anchored in the teacher's assets. This teacher's success gave Ravelle data to share with other teachers, inspiring them to adopt and expand her approach.

Here are the strengths and States of Being I captured in that session:

- Create a vision/philosophy
- Appreciate That Everyone Has a Piece of the Truth (Gather Perspectives)
- Research
- Have an end in mind
- Start small
- See the Higher Self (Coach to Assets)
- Be Present (Remain Unattached to Outcome)
- Create culturally relevant curriculum

- Collect data

- Communicate the Why

- Build community

We translated these strengths to working with discipline issues: She began with an end in mind—a transformational philosophy anchored in Bose's research to heal before teaching, then worked with a small reading group. She *remained unattached to the outcome* by focusing on teaching Dionne how to self-regulate rather than on getting him to behave or on shifting an entire culture. She adopted the perspective I offered to invite him to teach the protocol to the entire staff so he could share his new skills, or data. Ravelle and I worked interdependently. An outcome that we couldn't have predicted was that Dionne would be the one to help shift the culture through *offering his perspectives.*

COACHING MODEL

WHAT: Appreciate That Everyone Has a Piece of the Truth

WHY: There are many parts to the story the leader tells us. One of the challenges of one-on-one coaching is that we primarily hear the voice and perceptions of the person we coach. This can limit our understanding and scope of the dynamics that the leader engages in on a daily basis, and can make it easy to see only his point of view in the story. We can run the risk of taking the leader's side in conflicts, for example, or seeing particular colleagues only through the leader's eyes. Our job is to help leaders consider the larger story—their colleagues, students, and families' points of views, insights, and wisdom. Coaches also hold perspectives that can add to the leader's tool box as well. These have to be skillfully offered without telling the leader what to do, unless he is truly stuck, is on a deadline, or in a crisis.

HOW: Gather Perspectives

Begin with Self
- Before your session: Imagine the person at moments when you saw or heard him succeeding.
- Inhale *listen* / exhale *compassion*.
- Begin the session with See the Higher Self (Coach to Assets)
- Throughout the session, notice your own feelings and silently name them in order to manage them. Notice your breathing and other cues that indicate you might be feeling distracted, stressed, or triggered, so that you can *quiet your ego* and *be present* to the leader. Intentional breathing, shifting your position in the chair, and placing both feet on the floor can help you reset.

With the Leader
In person: Notice unspoken cues and facial expressions. Listen to word choice, tone, pauses, and breathing. Adapt your own listening cues through easy eye contact and natural, responsive gestures and/or facial expressions.

By phone: Listen to word choice, tone, pauses, breathing, and other vocal sounds that you have learned about how the leader processes. Offer your own occasional responses to help the leader know you are listening.

- Wait through silences to allow for processing time.
- Try not to interrupt unless the leader gets stuck in a pattern.

Be Curious

Ask nonjudgmental questions to listen for opportunities for others' perspectives.

Examples of questions or statements to gather perspectives:
- "What is your leadership team's perspective?"
- "Have you talked with a novice teacher and a seasoned teacher about how this decision will impact their teaching?"
- "How might _____ describe the situation?" (If the leader says, "I don't know," ask, "If you did know, what would you say?")
- "Which colleagues might have input to help you think about this?"
- "As you make new policy decisions that will impact the community, what are your community leaders' suggestions?" (This approach helps leaders think beyond the school's doors.)
- "As you make this new policy decision, what steps have you taken to discover how it might affect families?" (Examples: When leaders shift the time the school day begins or ends. Or hold parent-teacher conferences only during the workday, which can affect hourly-wage workers.)
- "This sounds like an opportunity for student input."

Interrupt Patterns

Healthy schools operate best, and leaders stay on the job longer, when knowledge is shared and leadership is distributed.

Example of interrupting patterns by asking a question:
- "What keeps you from getting input from your colleagues (or families/community members) about this?"

Examples of interrupting patterns by making a bold statement:
- "You've been down this path before—trying to do everything yourself."
- "I hear your pattern of needing to be in control, rather than having oversight or delegating."

Example of interrupting patterns by making a bold statement followed by asking a question:
- "Your pattern is to try to do everything yourself. What is clearer to you about that now?"

Imbue Others and Connect the Dots
- Appreciate the leader's knowledge and experience.
- Offer research, resources, and wisdom through other coaches, leaders, teachers, and experts who have experience with the same kind of challenging situations.
- Help him connect the dots.

Example of connecting the dots:
- "The last time you engaged families in planning the evening, the event exceeded your dream of it. What strengths did you use that you can call on for this gathering?"

Supporting States of Being
- Honor Story (Listen)
- Interrupt Patterns (Notice Repetition)
- Be Curious (Ask Nonjudgmental Questions)
- Be Bold (Hold Their Hand While You Hold Their Feet to the Fire)
- Imbue Others with Their Own Intelligence (Help Them Connect the Dots)

Potential Traps
- Certainty that there is only one right solution
- Believing that progress only comes from telling rather than asking
- Being impatient
- Focusing only on results
- Considering only the leader's point of view
- Leading with ego

Chapter 12

Imbue Others with Their Own Intelligence
Help Them Connect the Dots

You see you wouldn't ask why the rose that grew from the
concrete had
damaged petals
On the contrary, we would all celebrate its tenacity
We would all love its will to reach the sun
Well, we are the roses
This is the concrete
And these are my damaged petals.
Don't ask me why
[. . .]
Ask me how!

—Tupac Shakur

OFTEN, WHEN A PERSON FEELS unable to solve a problem, the sense of it expands into an unwieldy, amorphous mass. Sometimes, challenges seem overwhelming, making it difficult for a leader to see they have the tools to solve problems. A leader's assets or strengths are the gateway to helping them *connect the dots* between their experience and a problem they are trying to solve, or a transformation they are striving for. We have to resist the urge to tell them what to do because if we do, they will be back in our office next week with a similar but slightly different problem to solve, expecting us to solve it for them.

Discovery and imagination are key in coaching and learning, for the leader and for the coach. When we help leaders *connect the dots*, they learn how to solve many problems, take leadership and ownership, and we are able to *gather perspectives* by learning a lot about how they think and work.

Connecting the dots

When we *coach to assets*, we don't ask the leader why they succeeded; we ask what they did to make that happen. In other words, when we see a success—like the impossibility of Tupac Shakur's rose growing through concrete, or a leader teaching concrete steps that improve lesson-planning, we ask *how*, not *why*, just as Shakur instructs us. We celebrate the tenacity. When a leader presents the problem they are trying to solve as part of the *coach to assets* process, we *listen* to them unfold their story, *remain unattached to outcomes, quiet our egos,* and *trust our intuition.* Through this process I have discovered that, often, the challenge they first present shifts, once they've told their story. I'll ask, "Is the problem you want to solve still the same one you first presented?" This helps ensure that we are solving for the actual problem they discovered through the insights they uncovered through their story.

During coaching sessions, I listen for parenthetical phrases and utterances that emerge because in coaching, all talk is big talk. While big aha moments or breakthroughs can be instructive or even intoxicating, and seeking them can be seductive, sometimes the most poignant information comes embedded in an offhand comment the leader makes. It takes a commitment to listening for these moments, and a seasoned ear to know when to remove the parenthesis. Our job is to remind leaders of what they already know how to do, then apply and expand on it. Reviewing the leader's strengths before a coaching session through the good notes we take is a form of *gathering perspectives* from the leader's own life.

A Meditation on *Imbue Others with Their Own Intelligence*

"Deirdre," a leader who is successful at coaching teachers one-on-one, is trying to figure out how to build a more effective team that she leads. To gather data, I ask a series of questions: What does an effective team look like for you? Tell me about your team's strengths and complementary skills. What have you tried? What challenges you? I remind her, from my notes, of salient strengths she brings to the challenge. But she is still stymied by how to engage with her team.

I move to a more transformational way to investigate how Deirdre can build her team: We begin to explore experiences she's had outside of teaching or leading, so I can *help her connect the dots* from her past successes to her current team-building challenge.

I recall that Deirdre once mentioned in passing—in parenthesis—that she did theater in college, directing plays. I ask her, "What success, big or small, did you have when you directed plays in college? You had to work with a group of actors and crew, right?" After acknowledging that directing was a form a team building, she begins to describe a success she had. I capture the strengths, States of Being, and 7EQs that emerge from the story she unfolds. She recalls how as the director of a play, she brought the actors and crew together to hear her vision. They read the play together, discussed it, and *offered their own perspectives* on their characters. In turn, she offered resources for them to read to deepen their understanding of the play.

She met separately with the stage manager and lighting designer to *gather their perspectives*, then brought them together with the cast to communicate it. She made time for the diverse group to *tell their own stories* that shed light on the characters and their interpretation. During rehearsals, she set up improvisational experiences to give the actors opportunities to *access their intuition* and make deeper discoveries about their characters.

Here are the strengths I gleaned from her story:

- Have an end in mind

- Communicate the vision

- Plan

- Appreciate That Everyone Has a Piece of the Truth (Gather Perspectives)

- Create a sense of belonging

- Imbue Others with Their Own Intelligence (Help Them Connect the Dots)

- Honor Story (Listen)

- Offer resources

- Acknowledge Mystery (Trust Intuition)

- Foster creativity

I read these strengths back to her to make sure she understands how I derived them, and to see if I missed anything. She asks me why I wrote *create a sense of belonging*. I could have given her the reason, but instead I remind myself that in beneficial coaching relationships, the leader—not the coach—does the heavy lifting. In this State of Being I want to *imbue her with own intelligence* rather than encouraging her to depend on mine:

LB: Do you have an inclination about it?

DEIRDRE: No, I don't think I do.

LB: If you did know, what would you say?

(*Important note*: "If you did know, what would you say?" is the golden question when leaders say they don't know. I have discovered that asking this question distances them from their own ego [from their feelings], engages their imagination, and liberates them to access their thinking, as though they were talking about someone else.)

DEIRDRE: (pauses)

LB: (I wait through her silence.)

DEIRDRE: Well, maybe it's because I asked the actors to tell their stories? I think this helped them begin to see and hear each other, and helped develop a sense of trust. But I think what might have happened is that there was something each of them could relate to in each other's stories, and that seemed to surprise them. Until they heard each other's stories, they thought they had little in common. Hmmm...

LB: Yes! Storytelling is a time-honored way to create a sense of belonging.

LB: Can you think of other ways you fostered a sense of belonging? (I use silence here to give her an opportunity to ponder.)

DEIRDRE: Hmmm...No.

I read the strengths list again to prompt her, but she says she still can't make the connection. This time, I decide to offer an answer to her rather than continuing to ask her to figure it out. This decision was informed by her earlier response. She framed her answer as a question; used words like "I think," "maybe," "might," and "seemed" punctuated with "hmmm"; and was unable to identify more connections. My *intuition* told me that if I kept prompting her toward discovery, she would instead feel as if I were testing her rather than *imbuing* her. I wanted to build on the successful understanding of her first connection: the storytelling. Deciding to offer her an answer was also influenced by our ongoing work together. I have learned to *listen* for the changes in her voice. When the strength, quality, and tone shift to a tenuous sound, reflecting the paralyzing insecurity she can sometimes experience, I know it's time to shift my approach and offer her a few answers based on the strengths we identified so that I don't deepen her insecurity. It feels essential that we remain focused on *helping her connect the dots* to team-building so that she can plan tomorrow's meeting and feel strong and prepared.

> LB: I think that asking the lighting and set designers for their input, then bringing them together with the cast, also contributed to a sense of belonging. They each had an important production part to play that gave them a sense of purpose. Also, they could see how they were each integral to the process—to your vision—to a successful end in mind. Your theater experience offers you a lot of strengths toward helping you build your team. Do you see that?

> DEIRDRE: Yes. I'm beginning to now. I never made that connection before because directing plays and school leadership didn't seem to have much in common.

I hear her confidence begin to return as she takes ownership of the challenge. This makes it possible for me to ask her if she can see how to tap the strengths we uncovered in the list above and *connect the dots*. She realized she had been meeting only with the leadership team to make big decisions that affected the teachers who had to implement them. That was an easy fix: She would merge the leadership and teacher meetings when making these kinds of decisions.

For her next all-team meeting, Deirdre decided to focus on creating a sense of belonging. She would begin with the question, "Take us to a moment when you felt seen." She asked me for resources to help her identify other team-building exercises to help build trust. I included them with her coaching notes.

During this coaching session, Deirdre began to recover her confidence. She had rediscovered a familiar comfort zone by drawing on her leadership as a theater director. Deirdre was back doing the heavy lifting as she envisioned how to transform her theater directing experience into leading her team. Having the accruing list of strengths also gave us a clear roadmap to follow as part of her ongoing leadership development. During our next session, I will begin with, "Tell me a success, big or small, that you've had building your team." There are many instances where we can help the people we coach *connect the dots* of their life map to their work. We get there by asking them *how*.

COACHING MODEL

WHAT: Imbue Others with Their Own Intelligence

WHY: Sometimes, challenges seem overwhelming, making it difficult for the leader to see that they already have many of the tools and strengths needed to solve the problem. Coaching can help them re-discover this. Asking the leader to define the problem and reminding them of their strengths helps them regain their confidence. When we help them connect the dots from a previous success to the current challenge, a resolution begins to come into focus. Unless they are truly stranded, our role is to coach. We resist the urge to tell them what to do because if we do, they will be back next week with a similar problem to solve, expecting us to solve it for them. Discovery is key in coaching and learning. By coaching the leader to make connections, they will learn how to solve many other problems, take leadership and ownership, transfer the skill to others, and, in the process, we will learn a lot about how they think and work.

HOW: Help Them Connect the Dots

Begin with Self
- Before your session: Imagine the person at moments when you saw or heard them succeeding.
- Inhale *listen* / exhale *see the higher self*.
- Begin the session with See the Higher Self (Coach to Assets)
- Throughout the session, notice your own feelings and silently name them in order to manage them. Notice your breathing and other cues that indicate you might be feeling distracted, stressed, or triggered, so that you can *quiet your ego* and *be present* to the leader. Intentional breathing, shifting the position in your chair, and placing both feet on the floor can help you reset.

With the Leader
In person: Notice unspoken cues and facial expressions. Listen to word choice, tone, pauses, and breathing. Adapt your own listening cues

through easy eye contact and natural, responsive gestures and/or facial expressions.

By phone: Listen to word choice, tone, pauses, breathing, and other vocal sounds that you have learned about how the leader processes. Offer your own occasional responses to help the leader know you are listening.

- Wait through silences to allow for processing time.
- Try not to interrupt unless the leader gets stuck in a pattern.

Listen and Observe
Listen without interrupting. When a leader is overwhelmed, she might tell an unwieldy story, making it challenging to sort out the most salient issue(s). Listen for moments when her voice has stronger energy, when she becomes more animated or sits forward in her chair, or when she offers other aural and physical cues. These cues often present the thread or threads to pull on.

Example of statement informed by listening and observing:
- "I notice that your voice sounded stronger or had more energy when you talked about _____. Let's focus on that."

Example of statement informed by listening and observing followed by questions:
- "I notice that your hand gestures became very animated when you talked about _____. Does that observation of an energy shift feel accurate to you? Would it be helpful to explore this topic?"

Be Curious and Engage Strengths
- Ask nonjudgmental questions about how they resolved previous similar challenges.
- Remind them of their identified strengths.
- Help them connect the dots between previous experiences and the current challenge.

Example of engaging strengths and being curious:
- "Here is a list of some of your strengths we have identified over time. Which ones can you call on for this challenge/problem?"

Supporting States of Being
- See the Higher Self (Coach to Assets)
- Honor Story (Listen)
- Be Curious (Ask Nonjudgmental Questions)
- Be Present (Remain Unattached to Outcome)
- Appreciate That Everyone Has a Piece of the Truth (Gather Perspectives)
- Acknowledge Mystery (Trust Intuition)
- Quiet the Ego (Check In before Checking Out)

Potential Traps
- Being attached to outcome
- Believing that progress only comes from telling rather than asking
- Being impatient
- Viewing people as obstacles not allies

Coda

Fishes and Sharks, or a Knowing in Your Shoulder

We often wonder what happens to people years after our coaching relationship concludes. What happened to the words that hung in the air between us? Which ones evaporated into the ether, and which ones landed on each of us? Most of all, we hope that these leaders who trusted us are thriving. That they are becoming their highest selves. As I come to the end of this book, to find out, I check in with Julian six years after our final coaching session.

Our conversation feels familiar, easy, and natural. And, at the same time, there is something palpably different about the man I coached all those years ago—the one with a kind heart wrapped in self-doubt, the big man with big ideas searching for a way to manifest them. The first thing I notice is how animated he is.

LB: Your voice has a very different energy.

JULIAN: What's something that my mentor said early on to me? (referring to one of our coaching conversations) "When you are fully yourself in any space it allows others to do the same."

I have been exploring that ever since. I am very, very strong. A good person. A powerful person. I don't have to apologize for what my ancestors have given me. Another big shift: I have hope in doing the right thing because it's right. I look at this as a practice trial run for the rest of my life.

(In addition to the stronger rhythmic cadence in his voice, he also has the sound of someone in flow, linking one idea to the next, effortlessly, without concern for convention—a hallmark of confidence and creativity. It's as if he has been storing it all up waiting for the moment, or place to unleash it.)

LB: What else is clearer to you now?

JULIAN: What is the purpose of schools? I think of that question even more so than when we were together. That is the anchoring question that I keep coming back to in my work now. School should be a place where there is no unintended harm. (He then quotes words I have written): "It is essential that we seriously, intentionally, and continuously commit to the work of equity if we are going to help leaders create schools and continue to support communities that lift up our students and their families."

JULIAN: (continues) I found myself thinking about how my coaching has evolved. Is my approach relevant to their leadership? Interrupting, not reinforcing rugged individualism, but instead, are they aspiring to lead a school that is truly valuing social justice? The definition is no longer: you get a grade. Rather, we have a communal definition of success because that extends into the community. The school is an extension of the community. If they don't see it goes beyond school walls, they are destined to continue the legacy of test scores as success. Repeat, repeat, repeat. It's dishonest not to name it.

LB: Name it?

JULIAN: If we can't at least get to the harm that's been done then anti-racism is a term we can't use. Freedom is attainable. [...] You don't have to be a slave to the conditions of your life. [...] so leaders don't grow up with all the internalized issues. (He notes that he has come to understand that this is "on par with health.") We have to equip people with tools to find their own personal freedom.

LB: Mmmm. And how do you coach to that end in mind?

JULIAN: The tools are the States of Being. I wouldn't have been able to imagine those things were possible in what you created, and the need to couple it with issues of equity and self. Or that they were even necessary in coaching people.

[He says that the States of Being coaching model releases leaders from having to create their own model. He continues to riff on his evolution since our coaching relationship came to a close.]

JULIAN: Our work helped me remember I am human in addition to being a Black man, hetero. Not just a living response to people's stereotypes. Hypervigilance was a constant state. Our work helped me know that for the first time.

LB: Are there particular States of Being that speak to you?

JULIAN: *See people's higher self. Imbue people with their own intelligence.* I *love* that one. *Don't worry about the outcomes.* All of them (States of Being). Then, being able to reveal the tools and skills to them (leaders) so they can do it. It's exhilarating.

(He returns to describing the continuing evolution of his identity—defining his own sense and understanding of freedom.)

JULIAN: People of Color suffer tremendously because they can't get to that space of freedom. I carry that tension in every space even when not provoked. Anticipating is a knowing in your shoulder. For forty years, it's been self-preservation. I can't see a tree or be appreciative of a baby's laugh living like that. That's what prison is.

LB: (We sit in a familiar silence to give breathing room to this.) What's clearer to you now?

JULIAN: Equity and identity are rigorous and need to be addressed as rigorously as academics. There is a path: A reclaiming of power that every group has to go through to get out of victim mentality. I'm re-anchoring my identity.

(Julian then narrates a story that could be a scene in a film we've all seen: the one that brings the mystic to an ordinary moment just when the lead character needs him.)

JULIAN: I'm in DC at the train station. I'm at the bar with a sandwich and beer. An older Black gentleman sits near me. The bartender who seems to know him well says to him, "So, today is your last day at work." I don't talk to strangers but I'm in my zone. This is an older Black man. So I think to myself, ask him. And I say to him, "What's your biggest lesson?" The man says, "At some point, my family would ask me, How do you deal with sharks? I needed to get off defense and get on offense. They're the fish. I'm the shark." I think about this for a second and say, "I'm processing what you're saying." And then the man says, "Give me your email address. I'm going to ask you what imprint you are going to make." (Disbelief fills his voice.) And he did it! He emailed me!! Get off defense. Get back on offense. Be the shark. That's what he said. Blew my mind.

(Silence)

JULIAN: The hypervigilant voice is being replaced by humanity. I'm much more positive now. More comfortable being who I am wherever I am. Fear has diminished dramatically. The rage behind my eyes was so intense. It's at a level 5 now from 10. It feels better. I calibrate the rage and don't let it be paralyzing. Anger produces. Rage paralyzes. Despite everything, what you attempt to do defines your legacy. I want my own legacy.

LB: Any final thoughts?

JULIAN: I'm learning a lot.

Julian decided to apply for a doctoral program in social justice and asked me to write a recommendation. I am deeply heartened to know that he seems to be thriving.

What's Clearer to Me?

I am driven by a ferocious need to see the higher self in others, and the belief that coaching can help leaders infuse school culture with love, a sense of belonging, and dynamic teaching and learning. Where all who enter schools feel free to speak their truth. Where leaders, teachers, administrators, maintenance crews, cafeteria employees, bus drivers—anyone who touches students' lives—are steeped in the understanding that they are tending to students' souls and hearts, as well as their minds and intellect. That high impact schools prepare students for their imagined futures when rooted in compassion, culturally relevant teaching and learning, robust curiosity, and a working knowledge of child development. This is how students become their full, authentic bold selves. It is essential that we commit to this because, as the late Honorable Elijah E. Cummings reminds us, "Our children are the living messages we send to a future we will never see.

The question is how will we send them into that future. Will we rob them of their destiny? Will we rob them of their dreams?"

I recognize that coaching is hard work. It requires deep self-awareness and a constant monitoring of the self if we are to make sure that we are coaching to the leader's needs and aspirations and not our own. Coaching is hard work because, as I have come to understand, when we engage with others and enter their world through the intimacy of the relationship, the landscape keeps shifting. We have to be nimble. It's challenging to stay grounded in the leader's reality, not our own.

We need the States of Being in order to coach to *their* needs and not our own. To have an end in mind but *remain unattached to their outcome*, because outcomes can change. It can feel easier to be judgmental than to seek to understand or *be curious*, to give advice rather than *imbue the leader with her own intelligence*, or help her come to her own answers. It takes patience and humility to elicit and *listen to and honor story* rather than make assumptions through ego and arrogance.

I have deep admiration for leaders who embrace the States of Being and the 7EQs, or their equivalent. The practice is arduous because it requires rejecting the mythology about effective school leadership: that test scores are the marker of successful schools. That telling teachers what they do wrong will lead to effective teaching, when in practice, *coaching to their strengths* is what will propel them toward success. In fact, most of the leaders I have worked with over 25 years report that this concept is new to them—that in their experience, outcomes supersede process, which by definition can mean that test scores eclipse love, compassion, cultural relevance, and pedagogy. I have deep admiration for anyone who commits to the often brutal work of confronting their own biases, then committing to become anti-racist and anti-sexist.

It takes time, discipline, and courage to become adept at coaching to States of Being, to wrestle with the 7EQs, and to develop the dedicated practice to integrate them. While there has been progress on this front, the struggle continues. We are far from where we need to be. There are myriad reasons for this reality. There still aren't enough leaders or senior administrators of color in districts or in schools, or enough teachers of color. There is still not the same commitment to creating a sense of belonging in schools as there is to teaching math. School leaders who are fiercely committed to equity and to changing the culture in their schools—tending to their students' stories, keeping them emotionally or spiritually safe, and instilling in them a desire for lifelong learning instead of focusing on outcomes and grades—may find themselves out of a job, or transferred to another role, for not producing the results the local school boards want to see. It's a case of policy over people. Test scores still rule, punishment can be confused with consequences, and, in many instances, the work of equity is still seen as an add-on rather than integrated into a school's culture and curriculum.

What's clearer to me is that to create conditions for enduring structural and systemic change to occur, we need the courage to hold a clear, fierce vision and pursue it without distraction. Or fear. This requires us to live with dualities. Urgency and patience. Solitude and community. Confidence and insecurity.

One of the most challenging dualities in driving change is that speaking truth—especially to power—is necessary. And, it is dangerous. Speaking truth can marginalize us when we need to have wider access. It can deny promotions, and it can get us fired. But if we are clear about the difference between what is important and what is truly urgent, then we can be bold, strategic, and willing to take risks as leaders who are committed to an equitable and just society.

Finally, what's clearer to me is that big systemic, structural change begins one leader at a time, one room at a time, anchored in guiding principles of justice and equity, fueled by courage, and budgets that reflect values. It requires engaging the community in very deliberate ways, where all voices have value, where everyone has a piece of the truth, and where dissent occurs in safety, particularly when we are trying to shift a room that is intentionally and historically crooked.

Last Look

Dance
with the time
and the wind
and the light
Take wing
with the birds
Be fearless
Take flight

Acknowledgments

THE FIRST WORDS DR. RICHARD Streedain said to me 20 years ago were, "What's your favorite book about leadership?" I answered: "I'm afraid it's not one of the really well-known, commercial books. It's *Martin Luther King, Jr. on Leadership*." Without missing a beat he responded, "Oh, the Donald Phillips book! Excellent choice!" Ever since, Dick has been a loyal friend, colleague, and coach. There would be no dream of a book without him. With selfless enthusiasm, he pushed open doors that I never imagined were accessible to me—most especially the door to a doctoral degree at age 69. He has a bottomless backpack of scholarly books and articles and a seasoned fluency across the vast fields of education, psychology, philosophy, and the history of race and justice in the United States. He sees around corners that others don't yet know exist, is a quintessential connector, and is a lifelong, on-the-ground worker in the struggle for equity. Dick, the most optimistic and quietly generous person I have known, has been my champion every step of the winding way. Among other kindnesses, he and his wife Cheryl Streedain graciously provided me with the solitude of their Oregon Coast home, where I wrote a major portion of this book. I am deeply grateful.

Pam Moeller was my boss in 2000 for the first KIPP School Leadership Program where I was hired to lead one workshop. A little less than a decade later, we traded places; I became her boss as the founding director of the Leadership Coaching Program. We made our third and final shift in our working relationship in 2016 when I retired and she took the helm of the program. Somewhere in between those years, Pam encouraged me to codify my coaching process, which became the genesis for this book. She embraces and fiercely protects the States of Being as if they were her own, expanding and enriching the program beyond my wildest dreams. Every shift we have made has been fluid, respectful, and supportive. We continue to listen to each other's stories and coach each other toward becoming our highest selves. I believe we have helped pave the way for other women leaders to be their authentic selves, too.

I wish I could list the many hundreds of leaders and coaches I have had the privilege to work with over the years. We have taken each other to the edge many times, and I have emerged as a better coach and leader because of them. I am particularly grateful to the following coaching colleagues who, early on, extended their trust while we built a program together. They are intrepid, inspiring, honest, fiercely dedicated to making the world a just place, and to interrupting generational poverty through equitable education: Ellen Bhattacharyya, Keith Burnam, Daphane Carter, Melissa Gonzales Cassells, Ed Chang, Jessica Cunningham, April Goble, Stewart Hickman, Ryan Hill, Dr. Mahalia Hines, Marc Mannella, Vincent Marigna, Adam Meinig, Dr. Bill Olsen, Laura Bowen Pickard, Amy Pouba, Jeff Rutel, Shawadeim Reagans, Dr. Blanca Ruiz-Williams, Oliver Sicat, Quinton Vance, Shawna Wells, and Orpheus Williams.

To my generous, candid readers who helped make this a better book: Donnell K. Bailey, Laurie Brown, Eréndira Flores, Dr. James

Henderson, Kelly Wright Henrion, Jeana Marinelli, Pam Moeller, Dr. Gerald Steinacher, Dr. Dick Streedain, and Orpheus Williams.

I hold gratitude for the fellowships and residencies that have made my writing life possible, including the Bogliasco Foundation, the Weymouth Center for the Arts and Humanities, and the Wildacres Residency Program. Each, their own kind of paradise, offered the luxury and nourishment of solitude. In 2018, I finally had the opportunity to study with Naomi Shihab Nye, whose poetry I have integrated into nearly every school and corporate professional development for the past 25 years. She has graciously given me permission to include "You Have to Be Careful" (*Words under the Words*, 1995) in this book.

The late Mario Melodia and the late Peg Rogers were early influences who helped shaped who I have become. Mario, my childhood dance teacher/mentor, taught me humility and confidence as I struggled to perfect the triple pirouette, and how to rise to any challenge through the demands of performance. Peg, my boss (1968–72), modeled what a woman in leadership looks like. She schooled me in equity and community organizing, demonstrated that kindness and rigor can, and must, coexist, and taught me the transformational power of story. Peg pulled me back from the edge many times.

And finally, I thank my family, the inspiration for and champions of my circuitous life. My son, Adam Sobsey, has an unwavering discipline in his life of letters. An insatiable reader since early childhood, his writing is fueled by his adventurous outsider spirit whether he's dreaming up plays or writing about baseball, rock music, wine, or remote villages. He inspires me to sit down every day and confront the blank page. My daughter, Leah Sobsey, is an example of what a full, authentic woman can be. She charged after her dreams to become a successful artist, college professor, and author. Together, with her husband, artisan Scott Howell, they are raising and nurturing kind, curious, and funny twin sons, Lucas and Simon. I have learned grace and resilience from Leah, and the right to claim and pursue one's vision from both my children.

I have the great good fortune to have my editor and daughter-in-law be one and the same: Dr. Heather Mallory. She has been championing this journey with me from its beginnings as a doctoral dissertation to its transformation into a book. Her attention to detail, to a word, to the rhythm of a sentence, to accuracy, to the Oxford comma, to the integrity of meaning, and her deep commitment to the States of Being, have kept me motivated. There would be no dream made manifest—no published book—without her. I cherish our relationship and her abiding belief in me.

Jim Lee, my partner in life for 20 years, has given me unfettered freedom and uncomplicated support to pursue my work, writing, and dancing life, and whatever the insistent muse sends my way. His quiet ego, deep intellect, moral compass, and respect for accuracy, challenge and inspire me every day to become a better person and thinker. A scholar—he holds a Ph.D. in Communication—and constant learner, Jim understands the power of words and language, engaging with them carefully and respectfully to interrogate the truth and advocate for equity. He holds my stories in sacred trust. He is an artist and mentor to hundreds of formal and informal students, and to our six grandchildren. I am deeply grateful for our life together.

Bibliography

Aguilar, E. (2013). *The art of coaching: Effective strategies for school transformation*. San Francisco, CA: Jossey-Bass.

Aguilar, E. (2018) *Onward: Cultivating emotional resilience in educators*. San Francisco, CA: Jossey-Bass.

Arbinger Institute. (2002). *Leadership and self-deception: Getting out of the box*. San Francisco, CA: Berrett-Koehler.

Blad, E. (2014, April 9). More than half of students "engaged" in school, says poll. *Education Week*. Retrieved from http://www.edweek.org/ew/articles/2014/04/09/28gallup.h33.html

Block, P. (2009). *Community: The structure of belonging*. Oakland, CA: Berrett-Koehler.

Bolman, L., & Deal, T. (2010). *Reframing the path to school leadership: A guide for teachers and principals*. Thousand Oaks, CA: Corwin.

Bolte, A., Goschke, T., & Kuhl, J. (2003). Emotion and intuition: Effects of positive and negative mood on implicit judgments of semantic coherence. *Psychological Science, 14*(5), 416–421. doi: 10.1111/1467-9280.01456

Brienza, V. (2012). The 10 worst jobs of 2012: 4—Oil rig worker. Retrieved from http://www.careercast.com/content/10-worst-jobs-2012-4-oil-rig-worker

Burkhauser, S., Gates, S. M., Hamilton, L. S., & Ikemoto, G. S. (2012).

First-year principals in urban school districts: How actions and working conditions relate to outcomes. Santa Monica, CA: RAND Corporation.

Cage, J. (1959). Indeterminancy, (part one) [Audio file]. Retrieved from http://www.youtube.com/watch?v=AJMekwS6b9U

Capra, F. (1975). *The Tao of physics: An exploration of the parallels between modern physics and Eastern mysticism.* Boston, MA: Shambhala.

Carolina Friends School. (n.d.). Mission and philosophy. Retrieved from http://www.cfsnc.org/page.cfm?p=593

Chapman, G. D., & White, P. E. (2012). *The 5 languages of appreciation in the workplace: Empowering organizations by encouraging people.* Chicago, IL: Northfield.

Chopra, D. (2010). *The soul of leadership: Unlocking your potential.* New York, NY: Harmony Books.

Covey, S. R. (2010). Foreword. In A. N. Pattakos, *Prisoners of our thoughts: Viktor Frankl's principles for discovering meaning in life and work* (2nd ed., pp. v–xi). San Francisco, CA: Berrett-Koehler.

Crenshaw, K., Ocen, P., & Nanda, J. (2015). Black girls matter: Pushed out, overpoliced, and underprotected. New York, NY: African American Policy Forum and Center for Intersectionality and Social Policy Studies. Retrieved from https://www.law.columbia.edu/sites/default/files/legacy/files/public_affairs/2015/february_2015/black_girls_matter_report_2.4.15.pdf

Didion, J. (2006). *We tell ourselves stories in order to live.* New York, NY: Knopf.

Doll, A., Hölzel, B., Bratec, S., Boucard, C., Xie, X., Wohlschläger, A., & Sorg, C. (2016). Mindful attention to breath regulates emotions via increased amygdala–prefrontal cortex connectivity. *NeuroImage,*134, 305–313. doi.org/10.1016/j.neuroimage.2016.03.041.

Dorrance, A. (2002). *The vision of a champion: Advice and inspiration from the world's most successful women's soccer coach.* Chelsea, MI: Sleeping Bear Press.

Dweck, C. (2006). *Mindset: The new psychology.* New York, NY: Ballantine Books.

Dyer, K. (2000). *The intuitive principal: A guide to leadership*. Thousand Oaks, CA: Corwin Press.

EdBuild. (n.d.) Nonwhite school districts get $23 million less than white districts. Retrieved from https://edbuild.org/content/23-billion#CA

Einstein, A. (1950, February 12). [Letter to Robert S. Marcus]. Retrieved from http://www.lettersofnote.com/2011/11/delusion.html

Elkind, D. (1981). *The hurried child*. Boston, MA: DeCapo Press.

Emmons, R., & McCullough, M. E. (2004). *The psychology of gratitude*. New York, NY: Oxford University Press.

Enayati, A. (2012, June 1). The importance of belonging. CNN Health. Retrieved from https://www.cnn.com/2012/06/01/health/enayati-importance-of-belonging/index.html

Erickson, M. (2012, August 26). The neuroscience of creativity and insight. *Big Think*. Retrieved from http://bigthink.com/think-tank/eureka-the-neuroscience-of-creativity-insight

Eugene School District. (2012, November 12). Session three: District 4J principals with Dr. Jon Saphier. Retrieved from http://www.4j.lane.edu/2012/11/session-three- district-4j-principals-with-dr-jon-saphier/

Frank, J., Bose, B., & Schrobenhauser-Clonan, A. (2014). Effectiveness of a school-based yoga program on adolescent mental health, stress coping strategies, and attitudes toward violence. *Journal of Applied School Psychology, 30*(1), 29–49. doi: 10.1080/15377903.2013.863259

Frank, J., (n.d.). Results of Transformative Life Skills (TLS) evaluation. Independent Research conducted in conjunction with Pennsylvania State University Prevention Research Center. Retrieved from Niroga Institute website: http://www.niroga.org/research/pdf/frank-tls_eval-v2.pdf

Frankl, V. (1946). *Man's search for meaning*. Boston, MA: Beacon Press. 130

Fullan, M. (2001). *Leading a culture of change*. San Francisco, CA: Jossey-Bass.

Fullan, M. (2003). *The moral imperative of school leadership*. Thousand Oaks, CA: Corwin Press.

Gallup releases new insights into the state of American schools. (2014, April 10). *The Gallup Blog*. Retrieved from http://thegallupblog.gallup.com/2014/04/gallup- releases-new-insights-into-state.html

Garten, A. (2011, September). Know thyself with a brain scan [Video file]. TEDxToronto. Retrieved from http://www.ted.com/talks/lang/en/ariel_garten_know_thyself_with_a_brain_scanner. html

Gay, C. (2000). *Culturally responsive teaching: Theory, research, and practice.* New York, NY: Teachers College Press.

Gibson, H. V. (2010). *Improving academic achievement for Black male students: Portraits of successful teachers' instructional approach and pedagogy* (Doctoral dissertation, Harvard University). Available from ProQuest Dissertations and Theses database (UMI No. 3446302).

Goleman, D. (2006). *Social intelligence: The new science of human relationships.* New York, NY: Bantam Books.

Gregoire, C. (2014, March 19). Ten things highly intuitive people do differently. *Huffington Post.* Retrieved from: http://www.huffingtonpost.com/2014/03/19/the- habits-of-highly-intu_n_4958778.html?utm_hp_ref=tw

Gutman, R. (2011, March). The hidden power of smiling [Video file]. TED2011. Retrieved from https://www.ted.com/talks/ron_gutman_the_hidden_power_of_smiling/transcript?language=en#t-360136

Gyllensten, K., & Palmer, S. (2007). The coaching relationship: An interpretive phenomenological analysis. *International Coaching Psychology Review, 2*(2), 168–177.

Haberman, M. (2004). *Teacher burnout in black and white.* Milwaukee, WI: Haberman Educational Foundation.

Haberman, M. (2010, September). Interview by L. Belans [Tape recording]. Conversations with Distinguished Educators. Available from https://www.lindabelans.com/haberman

Harris-Perry, M. (2011). *Sister citizen: Shame, stereotypes, and black women in America.* New Haven, CT: Yale University Press.

Headden, S. (2014). *Beginners in the classroom: What the changing demographics of teaching mean for schools, students, and society.* Stanford, CA: Carnegie Foundation for the Advancement of Teaching.

Heifetz, R. (1994). *Leadership without any easy answers.* Cambridge, MA: Harvard University Press.

Heneghan, L. (2007, September 10). Radical listening: Less talk, more leadership. Retrieved from http://www.jmw.com/assets/JMW_ Radical_Listening.pdf

Hermanns, W. & Einstein, A. (1983). *Einstein and the poet: In search of the cosmic man.* Wellesley, MA: Branden Press.

Hodges, T. (n.d.). Strengths-based development in practice. Retrieved from http://strengths.uark.edu/development-in-practice.pdf

Hughes, L. (1943, April). Freedom's plow. In *Opportunity: Journal of Negro life, 21*(2), 66–69.

Improvisation. (n.d.). *Wikipedia.* Retrieved November 7, 2014, from http://en.wikipedia.org/wiki/Improvisation

Jackson, P. (2013). *Eleven rings: The soul of success.* New York, NY: Penguin.

Jaffe, E. (2010). The psychological study of smiling. *Observer, 23*(10).

Johnson, S. (2019). *Where teachers thrive: Organizing schools for success.* Cambridge, MA: Harvard Education Press.

Kabat-Zinn, J. (2012). *Mindfulness for beginners: Reclaiming the present moment—and your life.* Boulder, CO: Sounds True.

Kegan, R. (1982). *The evolving self: Problem and process in human development.* Cambridge, MA: Harvard University Press.

Kerry, P., Grenny, J., Maxfield, D., & McMillan, R. (2007). *The influencer: The power to change anything.* New York, NY: McGraw Hill Vital Smarts.

Klimecki, O. M., Leiberg, S., Lamm, C., & Singer, T. (2013). Functional neural plasticity and associated changes in positive affect after compassion training. *Cerebral Cortex, 23*(7), 1552–1561. doi: 10.1093/ cercor/bhs142

Knight, J. (2008). *Coaching: Approaches and perspectives.* Thousand Oaks, CA: Corwin Press.

Knight, J. (2011). *Unmistakable impact.* Thousand Oaks, CA: Corwin Press.

Kotter, J. P. (2007). Leading change: Why transformation efforts fail. *Harvard Business Review, 85*(1), 96–103.

Kotter, J. P., & Cohen, D. S. (2002). *The heart of change: Real-life stories of how people change their organizations*. Boston, MA: Harvard Business School Press.

Ladson-Billings, G. (1994). *The dreamkeepers: Successful teachers of African American students*. San Francisco, CA: Jossey-Bass.

Ladson-Billings, G. (2000). Fighting for our lives: Preparing teachers to teach African American students. *Journal of Teacher Education, 51*(3), 206–214.

Ladson-Billings, G. (2001a). *Crossing over to Canaan: The journey of new teachers in diverse classrooms*. San Francisco, CA: Jossey-Bass.

Ladson-Billings, G. (2001b). Teaching and cultural competence: What does it take to be a successful teacher in a diverse classroom? *Rethinking Schools, 15*(4), 16–18.

Ladson-Billings, G. (2009, November). Interview by L. Belans [Tape recording]. Distinguished Educators Conversations. Available from https://www.lindabelans.com/ladson-billings

Lakoff, G. (2006, February 14). Simple framing. Originally published by Rockridge Institute; retrieved from http://www.cognitivepolicy-works.com/resource- center/frame-analysis-framing-tutorials/simple-framing/

Lamm, C., Meltzoff, A. N., & Decety, J. (2010). How do we empathize with someone who is not like us? A functional magnetic resonance imaging study. *Journal of Cognitive Neuroscience, 22*(2), 362–376.

Lawrence-Lightfoot, S. (2003). *The essential conversation: What parents and teachers can learn from each other*. New York, NY: Random House.

Lawrence-Lightfoot, S., &. Davis, J. H. (1997). *The art and science of portraiture*. San Francisco, CA: Jossey-Bass Publishers.

Lennox, A. (n.d.). Smithereens. On *Songs of mass destruction*. Retrieved from http://www.annielennox.com/lyrics/smithereens/

Lindeman, E. (1926). *The meaning of adult education*. New York, NY: New Republic.

Linsky, M., & Heifetz, R. (2002). *Leadership on the line: Staying alive to the dangers of leading*. Cambridge, MA: Harvard Business Review Press.

Logue, C. (1969). Come to the edge. In *New numbers*. London, United Kingdom: Jonathan Cape.

Marshall, K. (2010, January). Interview by L. Belans [Tape recording]. Distinguished Educators Conversations. Available from https://www.lindabelans.com/marshall

Matthew, R. (2008–2009). Transformative Life Skills Program. Program offered at the Alameda County Juvenile Justice Center.

McLaughlin, M. (1993). *What matters most in teachers' workplace conditions*. New York, NY: Teachers College Press.

Nieto, S. (2003). *What keeps teachers going?* New York, NY: Teachers College Press.

Niroga Institute. (n.d.). Research of yoga and TLS programs. Retrieved from http://www.niroga.org/research/index.php

Nye, N. S. (1995). You have to be careful. In *Words under the words*. Portland, OR: Far Corner Books.

Palmer, P. J. (1999). The grace of great things reclaiming the sacred in knowing, teaching, and learning. In S. Glazer (Ed.), *The heart of learning: Spirituality in Education* (pp 15–33). New York, NY: Tarcher/Penguin.

Palmer, P. J. (2009). *The courage to teach: Exploring the inner landscape of a teacher's life*. San Francisco, CA: Jossey-Bass.

Patton, M. Q. (2004). Heuristic inquiry. In M. S. Lewis-Beck, A. Bryman, & T. F. Liao (Eds.), *The SAGE encyclopedia of social science research methods*. Retrieved from http://srmo.sagepub.com/view/the-sage-encyclopedia-of-social-science-research- methods/n394.xml?rskey=20iCEn&row=1

Payne, C. (2008). *So much reform, so little change: Building level obstacles to urban school reform*. Cambridge, MA: Harvard Education Press.

Peterson, C. & Seligman, M. (2004). *Character strengths and virtues: A handbook and classification*. Washington, DC: American Psychological Association.

Piercy, M. (1982). A just anger. In *Circles on the water*. New York, NY: Alfred A. Knopf.

Pink, D. (2011). *Drive: The surprising truth about what motivates us*. New York, NY: Penguin.

Rath, T., & Conchie, B. (2008). *Strengths-based leadership*. New York, NY: Gallup Press.

Reiss, K. (2007). *Leadership coaching for educators: Bringing out the best in schools.* Thousand Oaks, CA: Corwin Press.

Saphier, J. (2010, February). Interview by L. Belans [Tape recording]. Conversations with Distinguished Educators. Available from https://www.lindabelans.com/saphier

Saphier, J. (2010–2012). Leadership Workshop. KIPP Emerging Leaders Professional Development. Chicago, New York, and Houston.

Saphier, J. (n.d.). Skillful leadership. Retrieved from Research for Better Teaching: http://www.rbteach.com/rbteach2/Skillful_Leadership.html

Saphier, J., Haley-Speca, M. A., & Gower, R. (2008). *The skillful leader: Building your teaching skills.* Acton, MA: Research for Better Teaching.

Scott, S. (2002). *Fierce conversations.* New York, NY: Berkley Publishing Company.

Seligman, M. (2002). *Authentic happiness: Using the new positive psychology to realize your potential for lasting fulfillment.* New York, NY: Free Press.

Senge, P., Roberts, C., Ross, R., Smith, B., & Kleiner, A. (1994). *The fifth discipline fieldbook: Strategies and tools for building a learning organization.* New York, NY: Doubleday.

Senge, P., & Wheatley, M. (2001, January 1). Changing how we work together. Interview by M. McLeod. *Shambhala Sun.*

Shakur, T. (2002). Mama's just a little girl. On *Better dayz.* Interscope Records.

Siegel, D. (2007). *The mindful brain: Reflection and attunement in the cultivation of well- being.* New York, NY: Norton.

Sorenson, S. (2014, Feb 20). How employees' strengths make your company stronger. *Gallup Business Journal.* Retrieved from http://businessjournal.gallup.com/content/167462/employees-strengths-company- stronger.aspx?ref=more

Stevenson, S. (2012, June 25). There's magic in your smile: How smiling affects your brain. Guest blog in R. Riggio's blog Cutting Edge Leadership. *Psychology Today.* Retrieved from http://www.psychologytoday.com/blog/cutting-edge- leadership/201206/there-s-magic-in-your-smile

Stiggins, R. (2010, March). Interview by L. Belans [Tape recording]. Distinguished Educators Conversations. Available from https://www.lindabelans.com/stiggins

Stone, D., & Heen, S. (2014). *Thanks for the feedback: The science and art of receiving feedback well.* New York, NY: Viking.

Tatum, B. (1992). Talking about race, learning about racism: The application of racial identity theory in the classroom. *Harvard Educational Review, 62*(1), 321–348.

Tatum, B. (2003). *Why are all the black kids sitting together in the cafeteria? And other conversations about race.* New York, NY: Basic Books.

Tschannen-Moran, M. (2001). Collaboration and the need for trust. *Educational Leadership, 39,* 308–331.

Tschannen-Moran, M. (2004). *Trust matters: Leadership for successful schools.* San Francisco, CA: Jossey-Bass.

Tschannen-Moran, M. (2009). Fostering teacher professionalism: The role of professional orientation and trust. *Educational Administration Quarterly, 45,* 217–247.

Tschannen-Moran, M. (2011). The coach and the evaluator. *Educational Leadership, 69*(2), 10–16.

Tschannen-Moran, M., & Tschannen-Moran, B. (2010). *Evocative coaching: transforming schools one conversation at a time.* San Francisco, CA: Jossey-Bass.

Tutu, D. (1999). Facing the truth. Interview by B. Moyers [Video recording]. Retrieved from http://billmoyers.com/2012/05/24/moyers-moment-1999-healing-through-truth- and-reconciliation/

Van Maele, D. F. (2014). *Trust relationships and school life: The influence of trust on learning, teaching, leading, and bridging.* Dordrecht, Netherlands: Springer Ebooks.

Vaughan, F. E. (1979). *Awakening intuition.* New York, NY: Anchor Books.

Wheatley, M. (1992). *Leadership and the new science: Learning about organization from an orderly universe.* San Francisco, CA: Berrett-Koehler.

Wheatley, M. (2009). Turning to one another. San Francisco, CA: Berrett-Koehler.

Willis, J. (2009). What you should know about your brain. *Educational Leadership*/ASCD, 1–3. Retrieved from http://www.ascd.org/ASCD/pdf/journals/ed_lead/el200912_willis.pdf

Yeats, W. B. (1902). *The Celtic twilight.* London, United Kingdom: A. H. Bullen. Retrieved from https://archive.org/details/celtictwilight-00yeatgoog

Made in the USA
Columbia, SC
22 October 2020